D0889083

THE LATER PHILOSOPHY

OF WITTGENSTEIN

THE
LATER PHILOSOPHY OF
WITTGENSTEIN

A SHORT INTRODUCTION
WITH AN EPILOGUE ON JOHN WISDOM

by

DAVID POLE

UNIVERSITY OF LONDON
THE ATHLONE PRESS

First published in 1958 *by*
THE ATHLONE PRESS
UNIVERSITY OF LONDON
at 2 *Gower Street London* WC1
Distributed by Constable & Co Ltd
12 *Orange Street, London* WC2

Canada
Oxford University Press
Toronto

U.S.A.
Oxford University Press Inc
New York

First printed in Great Britain by
Western Printing Services Ltd., Bristol
Reprinted by offset-lithography by Jarrold & Sons Ltd., Norwich

Contents

Abbreviations

PI   Ludwig Wittgenstein, *Philosophical Investigations*. Oxford, 1953.

       Note: the numbers (e.g. *PI*, 73) refer to the numbered passages in Part I. Page references are given to passages in Part II.

RFM   Ludwig Wittgenstein, *Remarks on the Foundations of Mathematics*. Oxford, 1956.

OM   John Wisdom, *Other Minds*. Oxford, 1952.

PP-A   John Wisdom, *Philosophy and Psycho-Analysis*. Oxford, 1953.

I

The Linguistic Approach to Philosophy

The greatest present single influence on English Philosophy is unquestionably that of Wittgenstein; his disciples and debtors are everywhere, yet his own work and thought are not easy for an outsider of the movement to approach. The doctrines of the latter part of his life, differing radically from those of his youth, were expounded only in lectures and circulated privately in typescript. His posthumous work, *Philosophical Investigations*, proves to be less a formal treatise than a commonplace book, or, as he himself calls it in the preface, a philosophical album of sketches and remarks. Other and easier philosophers who borrow from his ideas often adapt them freely: and he himself has been popularly portrayed as a kind of fanatic of subtlety—if not, worse, an addict of mystification. Despite all this I shall maintain that Wittgenstein's central ideas, like those of most thinkers of comparable stature, are essentially simple. Great subtlety in the application, the working out of an idea, is compatible with simplicity in its conception.

I shall seek first to present these central concepts in broad terms. It was Wittgenstein who directed the attention of modern philosophers to the study of language; though the elaboration of what would be called a 'Philosophy of Language' was, so he said, no part of his purpose. How well this disavowal agrees with the contents of his published writings may be disputed. But this at least is clear, that his own interest was not in language itself taken as a field of inquiry in its own right; it was in the roots of philosophical perplexity which he located there. Language, we may say, is the instrument of human purposes and needs; thus, very broadly, Wittgenstein thought of it. It is an instrument that functions variously, to various ends; for scientists and mathematicians, instructors and social reformers, even poets and punsters, employ language. Each works with it in his own way, and meets his own difficulties which he may or may not overcome. He may produce or fail to produce the sort of goods we expect from him. But the case of Philosophy is different; our concern here is not with the produce but rather with the instrument itself. The difficulties that philosophers meet are peculiarly obstinate and obscure; but in this they do not reflect any special intractability in the material we treat of. One may say that in a sense there is no material; that Philosophy has no subject-matter; it is the very instrument of our thinking that sets us our problems here. For here language itself is deranged; the machinery is out of order. The wheels revolve, the parts grind one against the other, they have all the appearance of working at full pressure; but nothing is produced.

The widely acknowledged strangeness of certain of the questions philosophers pose themselves, the paradoxical sound of many of their traditional doctrines, may give some colour, at least, to such a diagnosis. Something is wrong here—that is the suggestion. We must, however, look closer. To understand this breakdown of the machinery of language we must look first at its ordinary functioning; we must see language at work, with work to do. It is easy to think of human language as if it were some kind of gift of the gods, like Promethean fire; to give it a status that sets it apart from all the rest of our doings and concerns. Wittgenstein saw it differently. Language is part of the social behaviour of the species; it belongs as much to our natural history as walking, eating or drinking. It is created, or evolves, like an institution.[1] Parliaments and the party-system, social and religious ceremonies, cricket matches and competitive examinations are forms or functions of social life; and it is on these analogies that language is to be thought of. And they, in turn, may be compared to the hiving of bees and the nesting and migration of birds. Language presupposes, therefore, a non-linguistic context. It operates against a background of human needs in the setting of a natural environment. These together determine its character. And we must see it and understand it in this way, as involved in a pattern that goes further, if we are to understand it at all.

Our evolved natural languages are immeasurably complex. To command a clear view of their workings is, therefore, a matter of great difficulty. Wittgenstein accordingly makes use of certain artificial examples, by means of which simple patterns of linguistic activity can be exhibited in isolation. These he calls 'language-games'. The first example he gives is as follows.

> I send someone shopping. I give him a slip marked 'five red apples'. He takes the slip to the shopkeeper, who opens a drawer marked 'apples'; then he looks up the word 'red' in a table and finds a colour sample opposite it; then he says the series of cardinal numbers—I assume that he knows them by heart— up to the word 'five' and for each number he takes an apple of the same colour as the sample out of the drawer.[2]

What are we to learn from this example? Its full significance must be left to appear as we proceed; broadly, it is designed as an elementary model of a working language—to show us the character of language in little. What is asked of us here is to imagine no more than two people performing the actions described; how they came to do so need not concern us. It suffices that we can imagine it, and can appreciate well enough the sig-

[1] *PI*, 25; cf. 199.   [2] *PI*, 1.

nificance of the game; we can see how the words uttered function—the effects they combine to produce. And in all this there
is nothing mysterious; we are shown this, and *ex hypothesi*
there is nothing more to learn. Philosophers grasp at the essence
of meaning, the act of understanding, like objects hidden in a
well. Nothing is hidden here. So long as we only suppose a
supply of colour-charts and apples suitably located and can
imagine people behaving as these behave, the thing presents no
difficulty; and the whole performance lies bare before us. Yet it
is, or involves, a linguistic performance. What Wittgenstein
shows us, in effect, is a certain type of activity—the type we
call linguistic—interwoven with others, operating in certain
physical conditions, meeting human needs and demands.

One other feature of this game deserves mention before we
go on to another. To each word there is an appropriate response; at the word 'five' the shopkeeper runs over the series of
cardinal numbers, taking one apple for each; at the word 'red'
he matches the apples with the colour chart. The point to
notice here, however, is that the response is different in each
case. The parts of language are interconnected but infinitely
various in their functioning.

The second example is one that throws into prominence the
function of naming, with which, as we shall see, Wittgenstein
is much concerned. This game is designed to serve for com-
munication between a builder A and his assistant B.

A is building with building-stones: there are blocks, pillars,
slabs and beams. B has to pass the stones, and that in the order
in which A needs them. For this purpose they use a language
consisting of the words 'block','pillar','slab', 'beam'. A calls out;
—B brings the stone which he has learnt to bring at such–and–
such a call.[1]

Wittgenstein subsequently complicates this game by adding

[1] *PI*, 2.

the words 'this' and 'there'. The builder says 'this—there', pointing first to a stone and then to a place; the assistant carries the stone to the place. These simplified language-games admit of such complication indefinitely: the difference between them and a full-grown, natural language such as English is ultimately one of degree. In fact Wittgenstein applies the term 'language-game' not only to these artificial examples but also to any integrated set of usages, forming a complex within the body of a natural language. In this sense we may say that telling the time is a language-game. It is played in a certain context—that of our own position on the surface of the earth, and the revolution of the heavenly bodies—and thus presupposes certain physical conditions, much as the shopkeeper's game requires apples and colour-charts. And here we may briefly introduce a further point, one which will presently prove to be of great importance.

What we have been shown are performances in which several types of activity are interwoven. The relations between them are different in every case. Any one of these activities, however, might be performed, or something like it might be performed, in isolation from the rest—or from the physical conditions to which it belongs. The builder might say 'This—there!' and point nowhere. One might ask, 'Is it five o'clock on the sun?' —an example Wittgenstein uses in another connexion. The words now serve no purpose. They have the outward appearance of a move in the game but in fact, like a cog that has slipped, they fail to connect with the rest of the system; they are functionless. And in this they may be taken as a prototype of the questions that perplex us in Philosophy.

I have claimed that whatever the intricacy of the working out of Wittgenstein's method, the central conception is simple. His work was less an achievement of logical finesse than of imaginative power; what it involved was a re-orientation of vision. And the view of language that I have been sketching is surely not in itself a notably intricate one. But its application in any given instance, the laying bare of this or that complex within the working system of language, may certainly be more tortuous. Even here, perhaps, what is called for is as much insight, some sort of imaginative faculty, as theoretical acumen. For we seek, as Wittgenstein says, to command a clear view of the language-game before us—to see into its working.[1] I have said that we cannot hope to understand the dislocation of our linguistic machinery unless we first understand its right functioning.

With this we come to the core of the argument. I spoke of the breakdown of the machine. The metaphor that Wittgenstein himself prefers is of an engine running idle rather than working; or of a wheel spinning by itself in disconnexion from the rest of the mechanism.[2] Philosophical questions trouble and intrigue us. But the example I have taken, the question 'Is it five o'clock on the sun?', is transparently absurd, and does neither. It serves, just for that reason, as an illustration. Here it is easy to see what is wrong; the question fails in that it engages with nothing; it works nothing in the linguistic system which it claims to belong to. Language, Wittgenstein says, goes on holiday.

We must look briefly at a few living examples, to give some content to this general account. But there are two other points to touch on first. We have seen something of the working of language, how one part may fail to work, may fail to engage with the rest. The builder in the second game may say 'This—there!' with no gesture; and his assistant, no doubt, will stand and stare at him not knowing what to do; but here, as yet, there is no sort of problem, no confusion that calls for unravelling. For we imagined this particular game as being played—using it as an illustration without setting it in any further context;

[1] Cf. e.g. *PI*, 5, 109 and 122.   [2] Cf. *PI*, 136.

THE LINGUISTIC APPROACH TO PHILOSOPHY 7

we left it in isolation. But a natural language is a nexus of such games. If in some other related game, then, a move similar to this of the builder's occurs, and there has a real role to play, its vacuousness here may be less obvious. In these circumstances we might well look for an appropriate response, supposing that some such response must exist. 'What is the right thing to do when he does that?' we might ask. We might even suppose that we had found it, and following it thence into further consequences, pursue a whole labyrinth of blind alleys.

Here I come to the second point. Language, we said, goes on holiday; but also it drags us along with it. Wittgenstein was keenly aware of the force, the compulsive character of philosophical notions and doubts; they have the character of an illusion one cannot escape. The sub-systems within the system of language have got somehow deranged; planes seem to slant, dimensions cross. The impression arises in this way: in turning from one region of thought to another we carry over a whole set of pictures, for pictures govern much of our thinking. Our bewilderment takes on its peculiar character from the attempt to think not only in inappropriate terms, but in terms of inappropriate pictures. But here I come to my living examples which may perhaps serve to make this clearer.

Mathematicians work with infinite numbers; Euclid speaks of extensionless points. When we are not actually using or applying such concepts, they puzzle us. How is it possible to form the notion of an extensionless point? One tries, perhaps, to fix one's eyes on an imaginary dot on a piece of paper, and then to reduce it to nothing, while still, as it were, holding on to it. But then there will be nothing left for us to hold on to. All this however, this subjective performance, has nothing to do with Euclidean geometry. A child is taught that the shortest distance between two points is a straight line; with the help, perhaps, of one or two diagrams, he understands. Next he is shown theorems in which the axiom is used; and in due course he finds that he can prove them for himself. Proceeding in this way—and using all the while the notion of a point, which gives him no difficulty—he acquires a good command of the subject. He has learnt the language-game of Euclidean geometry; but the imaginative exercises I spoke of form no part of it. So too in the case of infinite numbers; we are apt to think of them, Wittgenstein says, as 'huge—only more so'. Here again our imagery is moving in the wrong dimension. The student of Mathematics learns a technique.

Confronted with problems of this sort, Wittgenstein remarks, we are sometimes beset with a feeling of giddiness; temporarily we are quite at a loss. 'What is time?' says St. Augustine, 'When I do not ask myself, I know.' This feeling may serve as our danger signal; it warns us that our frame of reference is misadjusted—and when that happens our world is apt to take on a surrealist look. Let us take another example. A philosopher writes, say, about perception, and we are led to reflect that visual experience is the product of a physiological process that terminates in the brain of the percipient. 'This', we say—meaning the room, or the 'visual room'—'is here', and we clasp our own foreheads.[1] A trick with distorting mirrors can produce a similar effect; the hall where we are standing seems to have been turned inside out, and understandably we feel a little giddy. But how are we to escape the illusion? I have already said: we must grasp the mechanism, we must achieve a position from which we command a clear view.

The significance of the present view of language may appear more clearly in contradistinction to others that it serves to replace; but we shall also be applying it in discussing them. The first sketch I have so far given may serve as some sort of guiding-line, so that we shall not get lost among the detail that

[1] Cf. *PI*, 412.

must follow. That, I think, sometimes happens to the reader of *Philosophical Investigations*; he lacks any landmarks to set his bearings by. At the same time it is important to bear in mind that Wittgenstein himself preferred to tackle particular problems as they arose; in general he seems to have preferred discussion to writing. The ordinary self-deprecating warning of expositors must be applied with special force here; Wittgenstein is really a thinker whom no such outline, no extended commentary even, can do justice to. For it is always in the detail, the accumulation and variation of examples in his hands, in his own handling of the material he amasses, that the weight of his thinking makes itself felt. They give it its pressure and quality. Philosophical problems, Wittgenstein said, have a character of depth; and we feel it in his own writings—yet with no hint of magniloquence in his style. I have spoken of the reputation which his work seems to have got for intricacy and obscurity; he is regarded as a formidable thinker. Certainly he is not easy; yet this is only one side of his character. He has too a kind of ingenuousness, a directness, that is equally characteristic of him. He comes to his problems equipped with the subtlety of a sophist, and confronts them with the naivety of a child. To this gift his writings owe their freshness—a quality more often vainly sought in a show of colloquialism and slang.

In extending our account of Wittgenstein's method, I have suggested that we shall also see something of its application. In fact the opening sections of *Philosophical Investigations* are devoted to a discussion of *naming*, and to a prolonged polemic directed against a certain atomistic view of language in which this concept is central. Wittgenstein is here engaged in extirpating the errors of his own youth—a task philosophers usually perform with a peculiar thoroughness and vigour. But it makes, perhaps, an unfortunate introduction; for the errors in question, if so they are, mean little or nothing to many readers. Relatively few philosophers are, or ever have been, logical atomists. The rest, finding themselves plunged into an intense struggle over obscure issues, may well think what they have run into is no more than a private broil which they have no need to involve themselves in.

The impression is false, though understandable. The view Wittgenstein is attacking is that which sees the working of language generally in terms of the function of naming. A name stands over against an object; in some such way, it is supposed, all significant language must be related to some independently existing entity. It is a picture which widely dominates philosophical thinking. It leads us to see the relation of language to reality as essentially uniform, as a relation of correspondence or confrontation.

Thus generalized the problem is one that, I imagine, philosophers of no school will dismiss as trivial; but we shall do well to follow Wittgenstein's discussion, and to examine the view in the form in which he himself previously held it. We should notice, however, that here, in Wittgenstein's present treatment, this problem is run together with another, not perhaps necessarily connected with it—the problem of simplicity or atomism, which arises out of the argument that every complex thing must be constituted of ultimately simple parts. But that too is a notion that has a considerable metaphysical history.

On the view Wittgenstein now repudiates, all ultimately meaningful elements of language must be such that they represent elements of reality; these will be what have been called logically proper names. The rest—such words as 'if', 'therefore' or 'and'—belong to the apparatus of language; they are part of what is called its logical syntax, but they do not represent reality. Such words as 'table' and 'beetle' may more plausibly be thought of as *quasi* names; but even they will hardly serve as they stand. Sentences in ordinary English may or may not be said to represent reality; but certainly we cannot, taking them in their present form, exhibit any one-one correlation between linguistic and ontological elements. That is what was sought, for otherwise we have not arrived at any truly non-equivocal names. It is supposed, therefore, that these ordinary modes of expression are only loose or telescoped equivalents of what might be said in an ideal form of language.

It may come to look [Wittgenstein writes, characterizing the view he wishes to disown] as if there were something like a final analysis of our forms of language, and so a *single* completely resolved form of every expression. That is, as if our usual forms of expression were, essentially, unanalysed; as if there were something hidden in them that had to be brought to light.[1]

Here, in this notion of a 'completely resolved form of every expression', the notion of atomic simples and the theory of names are brought together. The view is this: an atomic proposition by virtue of its structure mirrors exactly a simple relation between simples as they exist in the world. Further, all meaningful discourse, or all discourse in so far as it is meaningful, must be ultimately analysable into this form.[2]

Such an account may serve to bring out by contrast the character of the view that Wittgenstein later came to hold; the doctrine of language-games which we have been looking at. In the former, one and only one kind of relation is thought of as holding between meaningful language and reality, a kind of formal or structural parallelism. We are given a picture of the confrontation of formally identical structures. In the latter there are various patterns of activity—infinitely various, Witt-

[1] *PI* 91.
[2] I do not mean to imply that these few remarks accurately represent in all points Wittgenstein's own earlier doctrines; their interpretation is controversial. But the quotation seems to make it clear that it is some theory of the possibility of an ideal language that he has in mind in *Philosophical Investigations*.

genstein says—each involved, certainly, with physical things and human experiences, we may say with 'reality', but each involved in its own particular way.

Clearly the acceptance of the one account involves the rejection of the other; but Wittgenstein also seeks to show in detail, from his new position, the unworkability of the old one. He deals both with the demand for the analysis of the complex into simples and with the use of the name-relation that the theory makes.

His treatment of the former is in effect an application of the general doctrine. He seeks to show that, while the notion of an element has meaning in particular contexts in which it possesses a function, taken absolutely it has none; we are at a loss how to use it. Asked, say, the elements of which a chess board is made up, one would naturally answer by pointing to the black and white squares. Here one is thinking in spatial terms; these elements are parts of a surface. But one might also think differently; the squares are further analysable into the two elements of colour and shape. And a philosopher in search of simples cannot be content with what in any sense admits of further analysis. Moreover what we call the white squares are in fact generally cream, and this colour may be thought of as compounded of yellow and pure white. Yellow and pure white will now be our elements; we have adopted yet another point of view. And clearly the process has no limit. From another point of view, which may be equally valuable and legitimate— for how here do we judge of legitimacy?—one half of the board will be treated as one unit and the other as another.[1]

Now in the atomistic logical doctrine we have been speaking of, a name is thought of as an element of language. And the language-game played with bricks and slabs is designed to throw into prominence the function of naming. Two things

[1] Cf. *PI*, 46–8.

emerge from Wittgenstein's discussion of it: first, that the relation of a name to its *nominatum* is in fact very different from what logical atomists have supposed; and secondly, that once this relation is seen in its true light its simplicity ceases to be obvious.

That game which Wittgenstein described is in fact a kind of parody of logical atomism; he hints at this intention.[1] We have objects—bricks, slabs and pillars—and words correlated with them, one with each. But it seems that if it is to function as language, we require more than a static relation of confrontation; the language must be usable, it must work in relation to these objects. 'Slab' here is not a description but a command. Yet it is from linguistic activities such as these that our notion of the name-relation is drawn. The language-game might be used as a way of teaching children the names of things. Now, 'Slab', taken as equivalent to our 'Bring me a slab', is no longer naturally thought of as simple; it no longer merely denotes a simple object. And, what no doubt influences us as much, the corresponding English sentence consists of four words not one. But in fact whether or not it is appropriate to describe it as simple must depend on the context in which we are speaking, and the ends we have in view. We often give commands in a single word; we require a more elaborate verbal form only in certain circumstances. It is necessary to say, for instance, 'Bring me a slab', when 'Slab' alone might mean 'Take him a slab'. But no question of that distinction can arise in Wittgenstein's imaginary language-game.[2]

Lastly let us look at the character of names themselves. A name, according to the theory under discussion, is the meaningful form of word *par excellence*. But names, of course, have to be conferred; naming itself is a particular language-game— one which philosophers usually speak of as ostensive definition.

[1] Cf. *PI*, 48.   [2] Cf. *PI*, 19 and 20.

Now ostensive definition may seem to be a process whose significance is unambiguous and self-evident; a sound is simply correlated with an object. Children are taught it this way. 'That', one says, pointing, 'is an orang-outang.' And Adam, we may suppose, simply uttered the sound when the first of the species was brought before him.

What we have here is a particular nexus of sounds, gestures and objects; it is false, however, that all this is of itself unambiguously significant. One might point to the door and say 'Go!' Here the same performance has a totally different function. This is not an ostensive definition—and yet it might serve as one after a fashion; for one way of teaching the meaning of 'go' in the imperative might be this. If a mother points to the milk and says 'white' clearly the child may take 'white' to mean 'milk', and *vice versa*. There are different kinds of game to be learnt here which are by no means uniformly simple and self-evident. The child's error may be corrected, perhaps, by his mother's pointing in turn to the paper and the tablecloth, repeating the word—a fairly complex procedure whose significance has to be grasped. Again one might set objects in pairs as an ostensive definition of 'two'; one might even in certain cases find it the best way to give an ostensive definition to point to something strikingly different and say, 'That is *not* a such and such.'[1]

From all this there are various things that may be learnt. The variety of ways in which words acquire their meanings is reflected in the variety of their uses; the ways in which the forms of language may be meaningful are no less numerous.[2] We may recall the different responses of the shopkeeper to the two words 'five' and 'red' in the first language-game—the different things, as we may say, that he did with them. Secondly, as against the logical atomists, we see that naming is itself a

[1] Cf. *PI*, 33-4.   [2] Cf. *PI*, 10.

particular kind of linguistic activity—or rather, there is here a family of related activities. The use of language is not to be identified with the use of names, for we are already using language in giving and learning names. Further, the kind of relation in which names stand to the objects which they name, and that in which object-words in general—which we may be tempted to think of as names—stand to their objects, is neither simple nor uniform; nor is it intelligible apart from the various processes whereby their meaning is given them. Names have no unique status among words; and the idealized name-relation of the logical atomists has little connexion with the real part that object-words play in language.

I have remarked that the views under criticism are those of a relatively limited sect; they have never been more. Wittgenstein's arguments may nonetheless be given a much wider application; contemporary philosophers have found them serviceable in dealing with a whole range of problems. Wherever non-natural qualities, subsistent entities and the like, are invoked to vindicate the meaningfulness of forms of discourse, the same model is at work: we have a notion, Wittgenstein said, that the meaning of a word is a sort of object—that to every word there corresponds a meaning, related to it much as St. Paul's is related to the name 'St. Paul's'. Theories of truth and of meaning are, moreover, much bound up together; hence to see the picture at its clearest we may turn to an application of the correspondence theory of truth that is almost odd, or alarming, in its straightforwardness—and therefore sometimes suspect even among those who accept such views elsewhere without qualms—the doctrine of negative facts. Given that the fact, let us say, that the cat is on the mat corresponds to and verifies the true statement 'The cat is on the mat', it may be asked what fills this role vis-à-vis the statement 'The cat is not on the mat', when this latter is true. Nothing could more nicely or simply fill the gap than the negative fact that the cat is not on the mat. This answer, tidy and final as it seems, has, as I said, met with suspicion; but it does not concern us here to ask why. It will suffice to recall Wittgenstein's recommendation to seek, not for objects corresponding to words and sentences, but for their function in human life as parts of language.

I have said that the assimilation, conscious or unconscious, of meaning generally to the name-relation may be held responsible for erroneous theories—superfluous ones, rather—in all parts of philosophy. The word 'good', for instance, is presumably meaningful; any but the toughest philosopher, case-hardened to paradoxes, will feel obliged to say so. Yet it would seem that there is no quality to which we can point, as we might point to the colour of yellow objects to show what we meant by the word 'yellow'. Hence it has been thought by certain philosophers that a quality of a special sort, visible not to the eye but to the mind, is the true subject-matter of all discourse in which 'good' and its synonyms occur. (On a truly Wittgensteinian account, we shall see, the name-relation no more provides an adequate model of the meaningfulness of 'yellow' than of 'good': we may recall the use of the artificial word 'red' in the shopkeeper's language-game.) Yet another doctrine born of the same assumption is that of Platonic ideas; they have been brought in, in part certainly if not wholly, to provide meanings for such general terms as 'man' and 'justice'. And here as in the previous case, the opponents of the doctrine are commonly no less victims of the mistaken picture of meaning that it springs from than are its supporters; nominalists no less than realists. Both alike set out in search of the second term of the supposed dyadic relation of word and meaning, but while the one party finds it in a single subsistent universal the other finds it in a set of resembling particulars.

It is very necessary to distinguish Wittgenstein's own views from others that they superficially resemble. Much linguistic philosophy retains a strongly nominalist flavour; the Wittgensteinian story half-told can have no other consequence. Suppose that we criticize the model of the name-relation as applied to certain classes of words but say nothing of others; we insistently point out that terms such as 'good' or 'man' are not names, but give no special account of 'yellow' and the like. We shall then seemingly have left on our hands a universe in which particular things and their qualities are real, while the rest are merely *entia rationis*. That phrase, to be sure, is old-fashioned; and even 'logical construction', its later variant, will hardly serve the very revolutionary purposes of linguistic philosophers. But the phrases are changeable: even without them it may still be effectively argued that—much as a university is a logical construction out of its various colleges and institutions—so the mind is a logical construction out of behavioural dispositions (and perhaps a few twinges of feeling); or that when we speak of remembering or copying the referents of each of these words is a 'higher-order activity', which is in effect no more than an *ens rationis*. And the argument will broadly be that such terms as 'mind' or 'remember' need have no ontological correlate; for if we examine their functioning we shall see that they do not operate as names.

Examples might be multiplied. Words for motives, we are told, do not name mental occurrences; there are no particular events that answer to such terms as 'pride' or 'ambition'. Causal statements relating different facts do not refer to any real existents which we may be tempted to think of as causal rails, connecting events: they do not state facts at all, but serve rather as inference-tickets licensing our passage from one fact-statement to another. And all this, we see, is arguable on what may seem to be Wittgensteinian lines. But meanwhile those genuine fact-statements—such there must be—are passed by

without any similar criticism. The picture we are inevitably
left with is therefore one of a metaphysical bedrock of hard fact
on or with reference to which other language-forms operate:
inference-tickets, dispositional words, achievement words and
the rest collate or somehow move over these facts in their
various ways.[1] The form of the argument is, broadly, the
repudiation of a misapplication of the model of the name-
relation. But for Wittgenstein himself, we have seen, even
names themselves can only have meaning as functioning within
a larger system; there is no rock-bottom of discourse or facts.

There are other views or assumptions concerning language that
those of Wittgenstein's replace or dispense with. But we may
proceed as before, both using his philosophical method and at
the same time enlarging our account of it. The outcome of our
inquiry so far is condensed in a single saying of Wittgenstein's: 'For a large class of statements—though not all—in
which we employ the word "meaning" it can be defined thus:
the meaning of a word is its use in the language.'[2]

---

[1] Cf. Professor Hofstadter's lively and penetrating article 'Ryle's Category
Mistake', *Journal of Philosophy*, xlviii, 9 (1951). Hofstadter diagnoses Ryle's
complaint as a severe attack of Nominalism, and points out that 'facts' in his
account seem to figure as what is 'real and the only things that are real'. It may
yet be noted that the preference for combination above connexion, description
above explanation, which Hofstadter finds at the core of Nominalism—as it is
in Positivism too—survives, though transformed, in the later Wittgenstein.

[2] *PI*, 43. I take it that the other cases spoken of are those in which we use the
term 'meaning' to refer to those distinctive experiences or pictures which, as
Wittgenstein says, words often bring with them—that is, to intentional meaning.
Cf. below, pp. 20-1. Professor Findlay has insisted that Wittgenstein is suggesting here no more than one among different possible ways of thinking of meaning
(cf. his review of *Philosophical Investigations*, *Philosophy*, xxx (1955), p. 174).
Perhaps Wittgenstein himself would have said the same; but the remark is nonetheless more elusive than it seems. From one point of view it amounts to very
little; almost any philosopher, having given his own account of some subject
matter, might grant the possibility of others that would be different but not in-

THE LINGUISTIC APPROACH TO PHILOSOPHY

The equation of meaning and use, in the light of our previous discussion, will, I hope, not need much further explanation. If we are asked the meaning of any word—of the word
'red' say, in the shopkeeper's game—we must answer it by
exhibiting its function; we must show the kind of work that it
does. But here we seem to collide with another view of the
nature of meaning, and one which has been widely maintained.
Meaning is correlative to understanding; understanding is a
mental process—and one which is often instantaneous. Meaning, accordingly, is thought of as something given to the mind
or occurring in the consciousness of the intelligent subject; so
that outward performances, even speech, are consequent on
the inward understanding of meanings. This further notion of
meaning may be easily run together with those we have previously been discussing. Locke, for instance, finds it natural to
speak pretty generally of words as the names of ideas; the
names of general ideas, he says, are general words.[1] Here the
relation that confers meaning is still thought of as the name-
relation, the meaning of a word is still an object, but an inward
object. And this inward object, the idea, is something intrinsically intelligible; it is of its very nature a bearer of meaning.

The main objections to such a view are nowadays familiar,
not only from Wittgenstein's own writings but from those of

compatible. But what is more typical of Wittgensteinian philosophy is to deny
that it gives any 'account' of a subject matter at all. It merely suggests analogies
and points of view: 'See it this way . . . and now this . . .' I presume that it is
this approach rather that Findlay is hinting at. What strikes one about Wittgenstein's treatment of language, however, is that it never seems to be offered as no
more than a possibly helpful point of view; it is something much less nebulous
and non-committal than that. For from the general position, such consequences
as the impossibility of private languages are—to speak simply and accurately—
deduced. Further, no alternative equally valid view-point is even hinted at;
rather, alternatives are examined and deliberately eliminated.

[1] *Essay Concerning Human Understanding*, II, xi, 9.

other philosophers who have joined or followed him. Broadly it is argued that so long as a man uses a word rightly whenever need arises, and responds rightly to its use by other people, the occurrence or non-occurrence of such inward events as we have been speaking of—an inward act of understanding—is immaterial. That is a part of what Wittgenstein means, though not all, when he remarks, having described the first language-game—that of the shopper and the shopkeeper—that here nothing is hidden from us, it all lies open. They both understand the word 'red'; they use it rightly. Certainly it might happen that particular inward experiences always accompany the utterance of the word 'red', but let us suppose that they report no such experience. Can we then *a priori*, or simply on the strength of their right performance, lay it down that they must be either lying or deceived? Nor does the case seem to be much different where our own use of the English word 'red' is in question.

The understanding of the word 'red', it may be said, presupposes the ability to form images. Without some such image to compare it to, it would be impossible to recognize say, a red apple. Faced with this claim, Wittgenstein asks, simply and decisively, how one is first able to recognize the image. One brings an image with one, it seems, as one might bring a piece of red stuff to match. But then one will need another image to compare the first to, and so on indefinitely. Sooner or later we must reach the point at which we simply do the thing and get it right; as we said in the case of the shopkeeper's game, one simply acts in these ways.

It is true, certainly, that often words seem to have an atmosphere that goes with them. There is, one is tempted to say, such a thing as an 'if'-feeling, a feeling of hesitancy that belongs to the word. It is less plausible to suggest that that feeling invariably accompanies its occurrence in intelligent speech.

But that its right use would in any case not be dependent on this concomitant, that the significance of what one said would be unaffected by its absence, this, which is what concerns us here, seems fairly clear. If one says a word over to oneself a dozen times it begins to sound meaningless or strange. The experiment may serve to show us what the atmosphere of words amounts to. It is hard to think that its functioning in speech would be affected.

It is also true that many people make use of images and mental pictures. Choosing coverings for furniture, one might close one's eyes and try to visualize the colour of the curtains they were to go with; or in working out a problem one might visualize a diagram. But here the thing to observe is that the utility of such pictures owes nothing to their character as mental; a piece of the material which the curtains were made of, or a diagram on paper, would serve as well, and probably better. Here indeed we have mental occurrences, but not such as to fill the role required of them; their mental status does not make them, in some special sense, bearers of meaning. For whatever use such mental material can be put to, physical things will serve equally well.[1]

Yet physical objects as such have no meaning, and a diagram is merely a physical object. An arrow drawn on paper is no different in itself say, from a block of wood. It is a dead thing. Yet the arrow, we see, points, and the diagram speaks to us; they are objects endowed with meaning. Where we cannot find room for something whose reality we are sure of in the physical world, we are apt to assign it to the mental. Here, as in a diaphanous medium, all things are possible; here meaning dwells. But what in reality gives the object the life we feel it to have is its use. One piece of wood in itself is as good as another; but the one, perhaps, in virtue of the use we put it to, is a

[1] Cf. *PI*, 139 and 141.

footrule, and straightaway we look at it differently. A physical movement of the head or the shoulders becomes a nod or a shrug in the same way; and a mere sound also becomes a word.[1]

We see, then, that the use of mental images is in no way the essence of understanding. But the notion of understanding as some sort of inward act is a tenacious one, and has other roots as well. It is possible, for instance, to read a page aloud correctly without understanding it; and hence one naturally supposes that understanding must be something additional that goes with and guides the overt performance. One who reads without understanding will probably read with less expression, and he will certainly be unable to answer questions on what he has read afterwards. But surely, we wish to say, there is some further difference—which is also the crucial one.

The mental act, we said, guides the physical one. One might learn sounds by heart, and hold a printed page before one while repeating them. But where we read from the page we have the experience of being guided by the words; in the other it is lacking. So one is tempted to claim; but it would be truer to say that when we are merely repeating a lesson, while pretending to read, we have the experience of *not* being guided. We deliberately hold our eyes on the page, and feel the writing to be, as it were, intrusive. In other circumstances, where we read slowly, with some difficulty, the experience of being guided might arise, or again if we were copying a piece of writing and trying to reproduce the shape with exactitude. It is chiefly learners who have such feelings; in proportion to one's mastery of a technique, one's experience in the performance declines in prominence.

A child say, has not yet learnt to read properly. Perhaps he gets a word right by accident, but he will get the next wrong. Another time we say the same thing, but this time he gets the

[1] Cf. *PI*, 454.

second word right; and at first he is as surprised as we are at his success. And from there he goes on. It is not clear where the act of understanding first comes in; no doubt when he got odd words right here and there it was only luck; but it seems that we can hardly expect a black-and-white answer if we ask of the first words of the first series that he got right whether it was by luck or understanding. He was acquiring a skill. Perhaps the child concentrates, frowning, and says, 'd . . . r . . .' and then exclaims, 'drink!' He looks up questioningly, but not yet quite sure; an affirmative answer comes, and his smile broadens. Now he's pleased with himself. But ought he to be? At first he was not sure; and hence it must be doubtful whether we can say strictly that he understood what he was doing. One who understands must also know that he understands; for he has an idea or a meaning before his mind. And a meaning, it would seem, has no existence, no philosophical role, except in its intelligibility.

Let us ask what the child is really likely to have experienced. One may answer that he probably felt a certain tension, and what one might call an experience of groping; and then a relief of tension as he committed himself and uttered the word. He uttered it either still hesitantly, or with confidence; and this too is sensibly different. Or again, like an adult reading, he may have said it immediately and automatically, with no distinctive experience at all.[1]

And yet it is hard to escape the conviction that some kind of internal and intrinsically meaningful, or meaning-giving, occurrence takes place. Understanding often comes in a flash; it seems that something is revealed or presented in an instant. And that, surely, cannot be other than a strictly mental process; it cannot consist solely in right use or practice. If the meaning of a word is its use, understanding should be a matter of the

[1] Cf. *PI*, 151 and 169 ff.

more or less gradual acquisition of new behavioural patterns; rather, we may feel, a meaning dawns suddenly in the mind. And further, once that meaning has been given us, the mere physical performance is easy; we go on without hesitating. In view of this it may seem that there is no other account that can be given but that the inward achievement, the act of understanding, is what guides the performance and makes it possible.

These objections raise many far-reaching problems. Certainly these distinctive experiences occur, flashes of understanding and the like; Wittgenstein does not of course deny their occurrence. But it will be worth remarking too that they are often illusory. 'Now I understand,' one exclaims, after struggling with some technique or calculation, and then one goes on happily from that point. But it may also happen that one gets lost again. 'I didn't really understand; I only thought I had,' one may have to confess. What we are tempted to call 'the experience of understanding' might be roughly expressed in the words, 'Now I can go on from here!' It brings a sudden sense of command, a relaxing of tension and a self-confidence, which may or may not be well-founded.[1]

Suppose one is told to continue the series '4, 11, 18 . . .' One might pause, and then say to oneself, 'Ah, adding seven', and so go on. Or one might go on automatically, as one would in reciting the letters of the alphabet. Given more complicated series, we should all reach a point at which we would need to discover the formula in order to proceed. But to have the formula, it seems, is to have the whole thing in a nutshell. One carries it about in one's head, and applies it as occasion requires. The formula is meaningful; it shows us how to go on, like an arrow that points. But the arrow in itself is only a mark on paper; it has that significance for us inasmuch as we have learnt how to use it. One may think of understanding too, of

[1] Cf. *PI*, 205.

the inward act of which we have been speaking, as similar to such knowledge of a formula. Now supposing that we are in fact concerned here with a formula that a man repeats to himself, then we may give the same answer as we gave of the mental diagram that another inwardly consults. A physical thing, the formula on paper say, would also serve; it would be as useful to acquire the capacity to repeat the formula aloud, so long as one heard oneself repeat it, as to recall it purely mentally. The habit of repeating certain words, aloud or silently, is only a habit, and no more requires a special kind of occurrence, which can wrap a long process into an instant than the habit of repeating the five-times table. Any formula, moreover, admits of misapplication; and again whether one has it in one's head or on paper is immaterial. The difference between right and wrong, or between intelligent and non-intelligent, performance was to be explained by the presence or absence of an act of understanding; if such an act can occur and wrong performance still follow, the explanation is clearly inadequate. Hence it seems that these inward diagrams and utterances of formulae cannot serve to fill the vacant place. Accordingly, Wittgenstein says, we sublime the notion; we imagine some species of formula yet more inward and more ideal—the pure act of meaning, a wholly mental thing, that admits of no misunderstanding. It is in that essence, the meaning which the mind grasps, that the whole system which we have to understand is somehow packed. If we possess that we can go on and perform correctly.

It seems, then, that the act of understanding contains the whole system in little: all the subsequent moves are telescoped into it.[1] And yet if we require an act of understanding to see that series '4, 11, 18 . . .' is formed by adding seven—but for which it would be impossible to continue it correctly, unless by

[1] Cf. *PI*, 219 ff.

chance—it would then seem that to add seven to four to make eleven will also require an act of understanding. The steps only differ in difficulty; and Descartes in fact thought that at each step in a deduction a further intuition is necessary. But now, we are bound to ask, what has become of the compact system contained in a single act? For each separate step now requires its own separate act of understanding. And again if adding seven to four to make eleven requires such an act, we shall need another to add one to seven to make eight; or to continue the series '7, 8, 9, 10 . . .'[1]

'I see! I understand!' one exclaims, and goes on from that point without difficulty. Hence we suppose that in that moment all that followed was contained. Our error is to think of the expression 'I understand' on the analogy of expressions that merely describe or report a present experience, say, 'I felt a twinge of pain as you touched it.' And the misconstruction brings with it that picture which entraps us, which then we cannot get away from. But that language-game is different. One might take a decision in an instant; one might say, 'Let's play chess'—and go on accordingly. Yet here we have no inclination to think of the whole game of chess as somehow already present in the moment of decision. The exclamation 'Now I understand!' in this respect resembles the announcement of an intention—where one forms and discovers the intention in the act of announcing it. It may bring, indeed, a similar sense of mental clarification. 'I shall go,' one says; and thus one has decided.

And now finally, having some specimens of Wittgenstein's method before us, we may go back and review, and enlarge here and there, our general account of it. In Philosophy, if Wittgenstein is right, our aim must be to get a clear view of the working of language in any of its parts. Philosophy does

[1] Cf. *PI*, 213-14

not, like science, offer explanations or advance hypotheses; it discovers no new matters of fact. For here we are ignorant of nothing; rather we have lost our way among things we know. We need not discoveries but reminders.[1]

The uses of words are infinitely various: there are orders, questions and reports, prayers and recitations. We lose sight of their variousness and seek to assimilate them. Every word must have a meaning, we say; and then we suppose that this meaning is in all cases some sort of object related to the word, as St. Paul's is related to the name 'St. Paul's'. But in effect we have said no more, Wittgenstein urges, than if we should say that every tool in the tool-box has its use; the use in each case is different.[2] Philosophy lays bare the uses of language; it seeks no more than to exhibit their actual functioning. In this way, but not otherwise, we shall see our path through our perplexities. Philosophical convictions grip us with the force of compulsion, we cannot conceive of the possibility of taking another course. It is as if a man who has learnt some one way of doing, say, a dance or an acrobatic feat cannot unlearn the trick: however he sets about it, the same movements result. 'This must be so,' we say; 'An inward act of understanding must occur if we are to use words intelligently.' Wittgenstein tells us not to think but look.[3] Language functions here in this way, not in that. The 'must' reveals the force of preconception that blinds us to things before our eyes.

It is partly for this reason that Wittgenstein often bids us consider the situations in which our words were first learnt;[4] we shall see then what setting they belong to, what part they play in our lives. One may ask what difference the first introduction of a given word made to the pattern of activities it was brought into. In face of philosophical perplexities where the

[1] Cf. *PI*, 126 ff.
[3] *PI*, 66; cf. 101 and 140.
[2] Cf. *PI*, 11 ff.
[4] E.g. *PI*, p. 226.

usage of a word may lead us astray, we do well, therefore, to turn back to the situation that gave it its meaning. Indeed we may give it more if we please; we can form language in whatever way suits us. What Wittgenstein insists on is only this, that we must make clear what further meaning we are giving it, what role we now mean it to play. Here we touch on a last important point: for Wittgenstein there is no compulsion about the use of words. We suppose that their existing use obliges us to apply them in such ways in other contexts; we think that the meaning itself demands it. But we may use them as we like; and further they have no more meaning than we have found work for them to do. In face of a philosophical 'must', of some statement that we seem compelled to adopt, we shall ask to be shown its application—what connexions it makes and allows, what language-game it belongs to. 'What can I do with this?' is Wittgenstein's question.

To achieve his end, to wean us from our preconception and break the power of those pictures that have come to dominate our thinking, Wittgenstein also employs various imaginative devices. When philosophers are fixed to one model of linguistic functioning, he uses analogies or constructs imaginary language-games that exhibit others. He imagines tribes with strange practices, or worlds unlike our own where things behave strangely; where, in consequence, any language that might exist would naturally function very differently from ours. For we have seen that our words, like the imaginary words 'five' and 'red' in the shopkeeper's game, take their uses from the context in which they operate; and by placing them imaginatively in a wholly different setting the nature of that tie can be made plain. In all this Wittgenstein's general aim is to break up the rigidity of our terms of thought. But he disclaims any thesis of his own, he offers no doctrine. He merely describes the various workings of language and lays them before us.

II

Logic and Normative Language

We have seen that Wittgenstein constantly compares languages and parts of languages to games; and this is a comparison that serves his purpose in at least two ways. It serves him first in that a game is usually a form of social activity in which different players fill different roles; secondly in that games observe rules. I have spoken at some length of the first part of the analogy; we must now turn to the second.

Where rules or standards are recognized and have authority, practice is open to challenge, it can be condemned as irregular or wrong. And that, of course, holds good of discourse in general, of statements, and of the passage by inference from one statement to another. And the challenge must be met, if at all, by the appeal to certain principles or rules, to, it would be widely said, the principles of logic. There are various problems that Wittgenstein discusses in this connexion which, in the present chapter, we must seek to clarify. He seeks to determine, conformably with his general view of language, something of the status of logic, and to explain the *quasi* transcendence we are apt to ascribe to it. Logic, which is exact and admits of certainty, may be thought of as representing an ideal to which ordinary discourse more or less nearly approximates. Wittgenstein examines this notion, connecting it with those earlier doctrines of his own which we touched on in the previous chapter—the belief in philosophical analysis, and in analysis not simply as an occasional expedient but as capable of yielding some ultimately ideal form of language. Further, when we understand properly the nature of logical and linguistic rules, we shall see the limits beyond which the kind of challenge which I have spoken of, the demand for rational justification, cannot sensibly be pushed—limits which philosophers, with their search for first principles, have been prone to ignore.

The reader of *Philosophical Investigations* comes very frequently on the term 'grammar' used evidently otherwise than in its literal sense. In this extended sense it is part of the grammar of the word 'rod' that a rod must have a certain length, or of 'colour' that colours are visible: and Wittgenstein further describes his own activity as grammatical; he is offering, he says, grammatical notes.[1] To one familiar with positivist writing, or with Wittgenstein's own earlier work, all this will give no difficulty; others may find it more puzzling. A language, we have seen, is a pattern of activities governed by rules. Within these rules there must be room for various moves to be made; but in so far as it is a language at all certain limits are set. In cricket a bowler must deliver the ball from within the bowling crease and bowl (in England) not more than six balls successively. But he may bowl round or over the wicket; he may bowl half-volleys or long-hops, leg-breaks or googlies. Certainly his practice in these latter respects also admits of evaluation; it might be said that he was wrong to bowl just short of a length to such-and-such a batsman at a particular stage in the game. But that, clearly, is in quite a different way from that in which he would be wrong to bowl with a tennis ball. The game, we may say, has a certain structure; there are certain moves which a player is bound to make in so far as he is playing this game at all. Clearly it is always physically possible for him to do otherwise; but then there can be no appropriate response from the other players, no counter-move within the game to the would-be move that he has made. He may be playing a

[1] E.g. *PI*, 90 and 232.

different game of his own, which has its own rules; then the two make no contact.

Grammar, in Wittgenstein's sense, is the structure of language, or, seen differently, its system of rules. A rule, we said, is what we appeal to in cases of doubt, or in face of a challenge. In much positivist philosophy the words 'logic' and 'grammar' are used almost interchangeably; and it is to rules of logic that we appeal when our moves in the language-game are called in question. The law of excluded middle, for instance, is a principle of logic; but it is so, on the present view, inasmuch as the prediction of truth and falsity of the same proposition has no normal or accepted usage in our language. That this is so appears most clearly in the case of a command: let us suppose that someone says, 'Turn to the right and do not turn to the right.' The hearer can do nothing with this utterance; it has no role in the game, no significance attaches to it. It might, certainly, be given significance. One might, on hearing it, turn half-right, or perhaps turn and turn back again in rapid succession; but that is to do no more than to transfer to these sounds the function that belongs to certain other sounds at present. And the statement, 'He did and did not turn to the right', is in these respects no different from the command.

Logic marks the limits of the language-game; and it follows that logical statements are in a certain sense empty. They are, as we say, merely formal. If we are told say, that a chess-player will never move his king's bishop except to a white square, that is no prediction about the course of the game. It tells us no more than that he will observe the rules; it lays down what he must do so long as he is playing chess and not some other game with the same pieces. The statement that every object is either cubical or not cubical is equally uninformative; and yet, here too, we may appeal to it, and to similar statements, to impugn other people's linguistic practice or to justify our own.

Linguistic practice, however, is at best shifting and indeterminate; chess and cricket have rules formulated, clearly laid down; they are precise and explicit. We may then be led to suppose that the rules of language or reasoning have still to be properly formulated, that schematized logical principles represent the true forms that our ordinary expressions only strive after. In logic we have the paradigm of exactitude. Sometimes, Wittgenstein says, we compare our ordinary language to exact calculi, the one, we say, approximates to the other; and we may speak too of such a calculus as an ideal language. But here we are on the brink of a misconception. Such calculi are things we construct; language is something we inherit. The two are comparable in certain ways, but we go wrong if we see this as more than a comparison. For we are apt to fall victims to the notion that in the one we possess, or might possess, the perfect form or the essential structure of the other. The ideal essences of logic seem to shine through the cloudy medium of ordinary discourse.[1]

Wittgenstein ascribes several different sources to this mistaken picture—though his condensed exposition is perhaps rather suggestive than luminous. First, he maintains that we often operate with inappropriate standards of exactitude. If one is told to come punctually to dinner, it is inappropriate to apply the standards of the laboratory. Surely, we may argue, to measure in fractions of a second is more exact than to measure in minutes. Wittgenstein answers, in his favourite metaphor, that the engine is now running idle. These notions have no place here; they make no sense in a social situation. It would be a kind of anachronism to say that one guest arrived more punctually because he arrived two-thirds of a second earlier. It is obvious at once, if we let ourselves forget our Philosophy and picture the real situation in which the language-

[1] *PI*, 89 ff; cf. 102.

game is played, that if it were said, it could only be taken as a joke.[1]

Secondly, Wittgenstein speaks of the feeling that a rule which is not perfect, which leaves any gap still open, cannot really be a rule at all. I have said that we appeal to the rules in case of doubt; and no system of rules can meet in advance all doubts that might possibly arise. And when we first perceive this possibility, we are inclined to say that we have discovered or disclosed gaps in the existing rules; it seems that the system as it stands is incomplete. Yet a complete system, we suppose, must still be possible; indeed, unless all our reasoning is to be left in the end hanging in the air, it must exist. Its discovery is the great task of logic. But our views are mistaken. Exact instructions might be given for the use of an instrument; but that does not exclude the possibility of misinterpretation. We may supply precise explanations to go with the exact rules; the explanations in turn may be misunderstood. And the process has no end. It is clear that the demand for foolproof rules cannot be met; every rule has to be understood and applied, and may also be misapplied. A rule is properly formulated if it does its work in the context it was meant for. Our error is to ask for perfect and complete rules, as if they could be ideally formulated without reference to their use or their users.[2]

A third source of the belief in an ideal form of language Wittgenstein finds in the partial success of the method of philosophical analysis. That success leads us to believe that every sentence, as it stands say, in ordinary English, is essentially unanalysed, so that its true form has still to be found. But the utility of analysis has its limits. There are modes of expression which bring with them misleading associations and pictures which give rise to perplexity; and sometimes we find that it can be shown that these expressions are replaceable by others

[1] Cf. *PI*, 88.   [2] *PI*, 84-5; cf. 87.

which carry no such suggestion. Thus the perplexity is allayed; analysis has done its work. Yet we fall into a new and no less radical error if we are led to think that the latter modes of expression represent the true form, the reality of which the other was only the phenomenal manifestation. They are no more than equivalent modes of expression which, for certain rather limited purposes, have advantages the others lack.[1]

Wittgenstein in his investigation of Logic goes deep into various issues, but he does little to map out or distinguish the different veins he explores. The conception of a single completed logical system, uniquely and universally valid, is, it seems, broadly equated with that of a single ideal language. In either case the picture we fall into is the same: we conceive actual language like a cloudy medium, as obscurely shadowing forth those perfect and true forms of thought or discourse. But that, we may notice, is a picture that appears not only in the search for such a system but also more generally. For there are particular logical principles which we actually work with and already possess; and these too are conceived in this way. We have seen that if Wittgenstein is right the former is an illusory quest, the completed system can never be realized; but the latter, the particular rules, plainly cannot be so dismissed.

The truths of Logic and Mathematics are represented as dwelling in a region of their own. Lifted out of the flux of contingency, they subsist timelessly, visible only to the eye of pure reason. Yet no sooner have we relegated them to this height than we find ourselves obliged to recall them; we have to bring them down again. For what use can these existencies be, with all their purity, if they remain permanently laid up in heaven and never descend?—if we never meet them at dinner or in the drawing-room, where the affairs of common life are carried on. Logical principles are said to be the prin-

[1] *PI*, 90–1.

ciples of right reasoning, and we reason about things in the world.

We shall presently need to examine Wittgenstein's treatment of Mathematics in rather more detail. Meanwhile it will suffice to enlarge briefly on what has already been said as to logic. We have seen that we guide our linguistic practice by appeal to usage: the law of excluded middle, for instance, serves to remind or instruct us as to what moves are accepted within the game. It serves, therefore, as a standard; and a thing is a standard in virtue of the use it is put to. Here, as elsewhere, we must turn away from those images or pictures that come to dominate our thinking and attend to the use and actual functioning of words. The metre rod in Paris is merely a piece of metal; as such it is no different from other sublunary things. Its place is in the phenomenal world. Yet when once we make it our standard, in some sense we lift it out of the flux. It must be confessed that here we lack the courage of our conviction; and there are circumstances in which we should no doubt say that the rod had shrunk, rather than that the rest of the world had grown larger. But that is only to say that there are circumstances in which we would cease to treat it as a standard. *Qua* standard it is unshrinkable—in the sense in which the eternal truths are eternal. It makes no sense to speak of it as shrinking. Mathematical laws and logical laws serve as standards or rules. It is always possible for us to cease to use these standards and adopt others; what is impossible is that the rules themselves should be tried or condemned, in the way in which we may condemn the things that fall under them—as breaches of rule.

A further and more obscure view that Wittgenstein held concerning logic was that it is always, at least in some sense, arbitrary. When we arrive at those practices that themselves represent the rules we conform to, there is no further appeal we can make. We regulate our language in these and these ways. Certainly a child will be reproved for proceeding differently; and their systematic rejection is, in many cases, a notion that we find inconceivable. One may, therefore, if one wishes, deny that they are arbitrary; but the denial can have no more meaning than that.

But in dealing with arbitrariness of grammar Wittgenstein seems also to have meant to convey more than that. He sometimes speaks of grammatical forms as 'a mode of representation'. Our grammar, it seems, is the form in which we represent the world; it is like a scheme for a map which for different purposes might be drawn according to different projections. In itself, then, Grammar is a mere structure, and so far empty. The illusion we are prone to, according to Wittgenstein, is that of thinking of a grammatical structure as if it itself gave some sort of specification of existent objects. We think of it as though it were derived from some such object, perhaps like the shape of a hat derived from the block it was modelled on,—yet an object which, for some reason, we cannot present apart from this product. For clearly we cannot speak of things without employing some form of grammar. All he can propose here, Wittgenstein writes, is to give this tendency free play, to try to apply the picture, and see what it amounts to in application.[1]

Take any proposition such say, as that events necessarily occur in time. If we see this on the analogy of such a proposition as that fish only live in water, we may suppose ourselves to be making a very general statement about the world. Wittgenstein's point seems to be this: that in the latter case we can in some sense compare the proposition with the state of affairs, but in the former we cannot. For in any account of what we find in the world, we are bound still to use our present notion of an event—a temporal occurrence. And hence what we try to com-

[1] *PI*, 374; cf. 491 and also G. E. Moore's account of the lectures Wittgenstein gave in 1932 and 1933, in *Mind*, lxiii (1954), p. 299.

pare it to is something that it is already involved in. The argument seems to be exposed to the objection that what we ought to compare a factual proposition to is not another proposition but to the facts themselves. And this, in the interpretation under criticism, will be true of such widely general propositions as that events occur in time, no less than of particular ones such as that fish live in water. In each case we have a proposition with a certain structure and facts given independently to which it must be compared. Possibly the answer to that would be that the framing of any proposition already presupposes some structure, in terms of which it is framed. The content may then be compared to the facts, but not the structure; for the structure must be given before one can set about the comparison at all. Wittgenstein allows and even insists that there are alternative modes of projection or presentation, just as there are various forms of geometry. And it would seem that we might compare these with one another and estimate their relative merits. He would perhaps have allowed that we might, if some particular purpose was in view; one geometry might be applied for one purpose and another for another. What he would have denied, I suppose, is that we can estimate their merits in this one respect, as alternative pictures of the world. For to compare them in this way, we should need some way of describing the world which stood outside and above all the other modes—and indeed any mode—of presentation.

At least this much is clear, first that Wittgenstein distinguishes in some sense between the structural apparatus and the content of language; and secondly that he holds that philosophers are prone to the error of seeing the one in terms of the other. We make a picture of a grammatical structure, and take it for a picture of an independently existing reality. 'We predicate of the thing what lies in the method of representing it.[1]

[1] *PI*, 104.

In treating of the comparison of natural and ideal language, Wittgenstein, it may be recalled, speaks of the latter as systems that we ourselves construct. That is in general his view of Mathematics; he regards what are called mathematical truths not as things discovered by or revealed to us, but rather as constructions that we ourselves have created.[1] It seems that Wittgenstein's interest in Mathematics remained in some sense a focal point in his thinking. His treatment of ordinary verbal language-games requires, I believe, to be set beside it, and gains much in perspicuity in the comparison. But in entering on the subject, it is proper to add that Wittgenstein disclaimed any specialist knowledge of Mathematics; and further, that that of the present writer is still less.

The relevance of these mathematical issues will appear if we approach the subject by way of a question of a seemingly very different sort which the previous account invites. A language-game, we have seen, is constituted by a set of social practices, and these practices, differently regarded, are its rules. Now in Moral Philosophy there is an honourable fallacy, one of some antiquity and prestige, to which this position seems to be parallel. Moral principles, it has often been said, represent no more than social norms. And the familiar objection to this doctrine is that we can sensibly ask of any social practice or norm whether it itself is right or wrong. Ramsey told Wittgenstein that Logic is a normative science;[2] and Wittgenstein took this as pointing to the comparisons between natural languages and exact calculi. But Ethics is also a normative science, and we rarely make such comparisons there. Wittgenstein was unfortunately little interested in Ethics.

It is clearly possible to change existing linguistic practice; and one can sensibly claim that the innovation is better than

[1] 'The mathematician is an inventor, not a discoverer.' (*RFM*, i, 167.)
[2] Cf. *PI*, 81.

the accepted form. Wittgenstein's account seems to allow no appeal beyond existing practice, and we must ask how it is to accommodate this possibility I speak of. Ultimately, I believe, it cannot; it splits, I shall maintain, on this rock. But we must look more closely at his treatment of Mathematics if we are to do justice to the way in which he thought of the issues involved in the difficulty.

I have said that Mathematics for Wittgenstein is not in any sense a process of discovery. Broadly the view he takes is similar to that taken by many empirically minded philosophers. The sole facts to be discovered are, it is widely held, empirical facts; and what we call the truths of Mathematics are things not discovered but made. We are apt to think of them as being somehow already existent, already there; and this is the picture Wittgenstein opposes. Until we make them, he says, they do not exist.[1]

But although not empirical themselves, these language-forms are put to empirical uses, they serve practical purposes in the world; and that is their original *raison d'être*. Suppose that there are two apples on the table: clearly to say that when two more are added there will be four is to assert a particular matter of fact that might, empirically, be falsified. It is false, for instance, that two drops of water added to two others make four drops. But the strictly mathematical proposition that two plus two equals four is subject to no such hazards; it predicts nothing empirical, and no event can tell against it. Rather it is a schema for thinking with; and as such may be useful or otherwise, we may apply it or not apply it—these are the alternatives here. It is perhaps possible, for instance, to conceive of a world of wholly ethereal or fluent things, where quality melts into quality; there—even supposing there might still be language and speakers to use it—there would be little

[1] Cf. *RFM*, ii, 31.

use for our present techniques of addition. We form our mathematical concepts, Wittgenstein says, in accordance with our needs and interests in the world: 'they correspond to a particular way of dealing with situations'.[1] But to abandon them as unserviceable is still not to falsify or refute them. We have already seen something of the way in which certain language-forms, being set up as models, may seemingly be raised above contingency.

Broadly, I have said, this view is not peculiar to Wittgenstein or to the *Remarks on the Foundations of Mathematics*, though it may still be true for the most part that other philosophers who share it owe something, if not to that, then to the *Tractatus*. But Wittgenstein's later ideas go further: we may get nearer to what is characteristic in them by a consideration of mathematical proof, a theme to which he constantly returned. He clearly recognized, what other conventionalists have, it seems, failed to recognize, the seriousness of the problem that faced him: for how can we speak of proving a given formula, how can proof be either necessary or possible, if it—and all mathematical formulae—are things that our own fiat lays down ? It might in court be proved that an accused man was guilty of larceny; yet to say so would surely be nonsense if this proposition, 'X committed such-and-such a crime', were not true or false independently, but settled by the court's own legislation.

Wittgenstein compares a mathematical proof to a picture, and we may start from this analogy. In the *Tractatus* propositions are said to be pictures of facts: thus the statement, 'St. Peter's is a cruciform church', would stand in much the same relation to St. Peter's itself as the ground-plan of the building. It is not in this sense that a mathematical proof is called a picture; a proof is no sort of a replica of an independently existing state of affairs; rather it is a paradigm or a model. Let us

[1] *RFM*, v, 46.

first take an empirical illustration that may make the point clearer.

Suppose we have a problem not unlike a jigsaw puzzle; we wish, perhaps for some practical purpose, to know whether it is possible to fit a given set of objects of various shapes into a given frame. Clearly such problems arise. Now it is evident that a picture drawn on paper, showing an area appropriately divided, may serve to teach us the solution; it not only demonstrates the possibility, it also makes clear how the thing is to be done. Wittgenstein similarly draws a figure, which he calls a 'proof' that a rectangle can be formed from two triangles and two parallelograms.[1]

Such proofs, if we are to call them so, are also paradigms; we refer to them when we are in doubt how to proceed. We have already seen something of how logical laws serve to guide and regulate practice. But our first example still stands in need of further development; it lacks, as yet, the mark of a typically mathematical proof. For we have specified no more to our jig-saw problem than an arbitrary group of objects, and similarly a frame into which they are to be fitted. A picture drawn on paper was to show us how to do it; but that picture will serve for no more than the particular case. A mathematical demonstration is universal. Let us suppose, however, that these objects we are dealing with form some characteristic set, that sets of this sort are, for whatever reason, found repeatedly; and that the same is also true of the frame. We shall then naturally give them names: we call the set S and the frame F. Our picture will now serve to prove, universally, that an S can be contained in an F; and this proof has a permanent application. Lastly we need only recall what we have already said of the

[1] Cf. *RFM*, i, 80.

way in which logical laws are, as it were, raised above contingency, and we shall see how this proof may approach a truly mathematical character. That an S can be contained in an F may be made a matter of definition; in default of this property we shall not call any objects F's and S's. Then, for anyone who speaks in this language, the proposition must necessarily hold; the language might indeed be abandoned as useless, but the proposition could never be falsified.

This last point is crucial; though I have already spoken of it at some length, it will be well to go over it in the present context. When Wittgenstein offers a figure drawn on paper as a proof that a rectangle can be formed of two triangles and two parallelograms, it is not an empirical possibility that he is concerned with. We may, for instance, cut pieces of paper into these shapes; and of course it is true as a matter of fact that the shapes can be combined so as to form the figure in question. We may allow, further, that if this and similar empirical truths did not hold, Wittgenstein's 'proof' would be of little interest; we might choose to work with wholly different concepts and terms. Nevertheless the empirical possibility is not what the proof, in its strictly mathematical character, serves to establish; for empirical things might be otherwise, whereas mathematical propositions are necessary. We can conceive, strange as we might think it, that however closely or carefully we scrutinized our pieces of paper beforehand, we always found in the event that they failed to fit. We might attribute it to some queer optical trick, or say that the paper must have shrunk—thereby testifying our adherence to our present concepts. But a proposition proved mathematically is exposed to no such contingencies; and indeed it is part of the concept of a rectangle as we have it, that it may be formed in the manner described.

We prove, then, that certain figures stand in certain relations; but our concern is not with physical things but rather, we may say, with concepts. A mathematical proof, it appears, establishes that certain relations hold here between concepts. But our original claim was stronger, namely, that we create these relations and these concepts. How is this to be made good?

Let us see. Wittgenstein draws a second rectangle divided by an irregular line into two unequal areas.[1] Now might not this figure too be called a kind of proof?—for surely it serves to prove that a rectangle may be formed out of these two areas. We have no inclination to say so. The shapes are of no interest; it would seem strange to think of giving them  names. Yet merely as possible shapes they surely have no different status. Rather it is we who confer a status on certain shapes; we fix them and use them to think with. Thus in working with shapes we create our concepts.

At this point I shall seek to clarify what I take to be Wittgenstein's purpose by considering an error, a false picture, which we are apt to fall into: one that these geometrical examples perhaps foster—and indeed the metaphor I have used, that of conferring status, may have the same tendency. The process we have been speaking of might seem to be a kind of selection. There exists, it appears, an infinity of possible forms, either patterns of symbols or geometrical shapes, which are all by nature equal, and we select from among them, giving titles and status to some and not to others. But such talk envisages, or seems to envisage, a realm of pre-existent possibilities already, in some shadowy sense, actual: there dwell the forms of future thought, awaiting our summons from the void. Now in truth it is we who make mathematical forms. To be sure, they must be possible forms; but to say that is to add nothing significant. For our concern, once again, is not with empirical possibilities.

[1] Cf. *RFM*, i, 70.

If we were dealing with pieces of paper, seeking ways of fitting them together, then indeed we could specify a definite number of possibilities, and then, too, it would be sensible to talk of selecting one or other of these. But here nothing is excluded; and to say that we select from the infinity of *possible* forms— where in the nature of the case we could not describe anything that would be debarred from the selection—is simply to say that we make them. For there is nothing that we might not, in principle, have made or chosen. Thus we do not say that Shakespeare selected the play *Hamlet*, but that he created it. I have said that we normally proceed with an eye on our own practical interests and needs, and hence too on empirical possibilities; but the problem we are faced with in mathematics is essentially to decide what new forms to fashion. In a proof we win through to a decision—thus, Wittgenstein suggests, we should think of it.[1]

We decide, then, to adopt or commit ourselves to certain forms; we give names to triangles, parallelograms and the like, but not to irregular shapes like the English counties. This process of concept-construction is plainly not a merely arbitrary one. Hence, if we are not to think of it as any sort of copying or reproducing of the structure of an independent reality, it is natural to ask how it is guided: what makes us go one way rather than another? Part of the answer has already been given: we proceed with empirical considerations in view. Yet it may be that philosophers have been too ready to content themselves with that answer; for it is clear that when we reject the figure of a rectangle irregularly divided, and accept that of a rectangle divided into two triangles and two parallelograms, we need not be consciously concerned with the use to which either figure can be put. We adopt those we find imaginatively acceptable: it amounts to that. And a triangle is a memorable shape,

[1] *RFM*, ii, 27.

whereas Worcestershire, as a shape on the map merely, is not. I do not mean to suggest, however, that the two factors I have spoken of are wholly separable; at a deeper level the connexion with utility may remain. For empirically usable forms will be those the imagination can grasp—those, it might be said, in a different philosophical idiom, that are adapted to our faculties. We pick out those shapes we can work with and handle.

Certain forms leap to the eye and we give them names; thereby we establish our concepts. Now let us return to our account of mathematical proof. A proof leads us from one concept to another. And indeed we must say here precisely what we have said of the concepts themselves; in the proof the material is so arranged or presented as to make the passage in question seem inevitable. This, too, is a form that we naturally seize on; the proof fixes our minds in one direction.[1] Previously we compared a proof to a picture; Wittgenstein calls it a memorable picture. Thus one might pick out the Prime Minister in a crowd from a familiarity with the caricaturists' version of his features or, more specifically, his moustache. The concepts that Mathematics gives us may be thought of as images or stereotypes in terms of which we can look at the world; so equipped we can handle the material presented to us.

A proof, we said, leads us from one concept to another, but it also determines the concepts it leads to. It arranges the material in a memorable way, thus relating C_1 to C_2. But apart from this relation, it may be, C_2 itself would never have seemed memorable; this later concept would never have crystallized at all. And thus the process of mathematical thought creates its own concepts while it works with them. We should bear in mind that a concept in Pure Mathematics is constituted by the relations in which it stands; hence we cannot say what 'six' is or define it, apart from its being twice three, the square root of

[1]Cf. *RFM*, i, 78–9.

thirty-six, and so on. A proof serves to arrange the material so that certain relations force themselves inescapably on our minds; and these relations, in turn, will define the concepts that they relate. It may be helpful here to call to mind one of Wittgenstein's favourite illustrations, that of a puzzle-picture. We may suppose that we have before us a mere jumble of shapes, which suddenly reveals itself as a pattern: someone underlines this or that part of the picture with a gesture, directs our attention here or there, and then we discover, let us say, a system of loops and ellipses symmetrically arranged. What before, in our eyes, was perhaps the tail of a rather pot-bellied dragon, or else merely an arbitrary scrawl, appears now as a definite form in a system of such forms: it may be one half circle placed so as to balance another. The two forms stand in a certain relation, but it is only because we see the relation as we do that we see the forms as we do; this one is a half-circle, for us, only as being opposed and balanced by the other. The relation, then, gives them their character.

I have said that a proof compels or induces us to think along certain lines, to see the material before us in certain ways. Indeed we normally feel that it compels us. There is one general objection to logical conventionalism so simple and obvious that it is strange that neither its exponents nor its critics have spoken more of it. However valuable conventions may be, they are still things we can unmake at will. Now we never naturally think in this way of logic: we do not *feel* free to reject the conclusion of a valid inference. Wittgenstein is alone, I believe, among philosophers who share this approach, in doing justice to this difficulty. Indeed a great part of his mathematical work is devoted to wrestling with this feeling that we retain of the compulsiveness of these procedures, of what he calls the hardness of a logical 'must'.[1]

[1] Cf. e.g. *RFM*, i, 121.

The sense of compulsion is illusory; that is the first thing we must notice. One who has written '2 + 2' is, failing the compulsion of the teacher's cane, in no way compelled to write '4'.[1] He may write down whatever figure he pleases or make arbitrary marks or none at all. But so long as he is *adding*, it may be said, he must write '4'; and that is true. For otherwise we shall not call it adding. We have seen that if we are to play chess—to do what is now called playing chess—we must follow certain rules; but we are not therefore obliged to play chess or to invent games with this set of rules rather than that. When we pass by inference from one mathematical or logical proposition to another it seems inconceivable that we should do otherwise—though in fact there is no compulsion at all. It is, we have seen, the business of a mathematical proof so to present the material that our minds naturally move in one way. It is we who adopt the convention; but in so doing we may be deeply committed to it too. We feel it or see it as something inward and inescapable. Wittgenstein says that Mathematics creates essences; and an essence too, is normally thought of as an inward thing, as something deep. 'How is that to be squared with conventionalism?' it may be asked. That feeling, so Wittgenstein claims, expresses rather the depth of our need for the

---

[1] The qualification may be more important than it seems. It is said sometimes that the voice of one's parents or one's nurse lies behind the magisterial voice of conscience. Wittgenstein throws out the suggestion (*RFM*, v, 40) that the attitude we adopt to Mathematics—more especially to mathematical errors—arises first from the training we have received. (This important concept of an 'attitude' will be further elucidated below. Cf. pp. 54–5.) He does not enlarge on the remark, but I suppose him to mean something of this sort: we are trained to dismiss an error from consideration, an error, like a heretic, is damned. But it would perhaps be possible to teach a kind of would-be Mathematics rather as Art is taught at present: we would encourage individuality and diversity, make much of 'free expression'. There is, I believe, a distinguished philosopher who reports that as a child he felt instinctively that 0×3 should equal 3. In most schools at present feelings of this sort would be frowned on.

convention.[1] It is built into the structure of our lives; and indeed we have already seen how the language we use always operates in a wider setting, how it reflects our different interests and needs. Another brief and characteristically vivid example of Wittgenstein's makes the general point clearer. 'All', he says, is a fundamental concept in our language, and we have a single word for it; but there is no single word for 'all but one', nor yet any characteristic gesture.[2] What Wittgenstein understands by the need for a convention will be clear if we consider the possibility of a language in which the reverse held. Such a language would not be merely inconvenient; it would go against the whole bent of our minds. Perhaps, too, it is something still more deeply implanted in our nature, reflecting our practical needs, that makes us seize on squares, triangles and parallelograms and the like, on figures we can recognize and reproduce; in creating mathematical concepts we set up interrelations we can handle.

What we have said of the apparent compulsiveness of mathematical procedures and laws has a bearing, too, on our previous discussion of understanding. We shall do well to recall the conclusions we reached in Chapter I, for each discussion throws light on the other. We saw there that understanding expresses itself primarily in right practice; for if a man can proceed correctly with an argument or a calculation it is natural to say that he understands it. And we proceed correctly, without hesitation, when we have mastered a technique.[3] But the picture which we are apt to fall into is of an inward or mental act of understanding upon which correct practice is consequent. And hence we are apt to suppose that understanding consists in the possession of certain private exemplars or models: having once grasped the principle, it seems, we are able thenceforth to go forward keeping that in

[1] Cf. *RFM*, i, 74.   [2] *RFM*, i, 15.   [3] Cf. *PI*, 199.

our minds and referring to it at need. The inward act of understanding, on this view, serves to regulate or direct subsequent
conduct.

The truth is rather, according to Wittgenstein, that we have
been trained to respond in certain ways to certain kinds of
situation.[1] We are taught a certain procedure or rule of action;
and so long as we rely on the rule we have no need to hesitate
or reflect. That indeed will be a great part of the point of the
training. In this sense, Wittgenstein says, we follow the rule
blindly. That that is so is a matter of grammar: for so long as
we pause and reflect, re-assessing the situation for ourselves,
it can no longer be said that we are merely obeying the rule.[2]
While we accept the authority of a rule, we proceed automatically and ask no questions. It is clear that such training will
often go pretty deep; it may well come to seem to us that a
given way of proceeding is not only advisable but obligatory.
Indeed if the possibility of doubt remained open, the training
would have failed in its effect. Faced with someone differently
trained, we can only say helplessly, 'Can't you see? . . .'[3]

Wittgenstein's general aim in treating this sense of compulsiveness that attaches to mathematical procedures is to free
us from what he regards as false pictures. One part of a mathematical system does not determine another like a piston-rod
moving in a machine.[4] We make these things, and in a sense
we may make them as we please, though they seem to stand in
authority over us. Wittgenstein constantly envisages systems
and uses of language widely different from our own—and yet,
though different, not inconceivable. Indeed there are limits,
for unless the procedures in question observe some sort of
order and method then, grammatically, they cannot be languages; we shall not call them so. But even that limitation is
not something we can think of as compulsive.

[1] *PI*, 206.　　[2] Cf. *PI*, 219–20.　　[3] Cf. *PI*, 231.　　[4] *RFM*, i, 199 ff.

At this point we may usefully turn back from Mathematics to ordinary language and examine another example of Wittgenstein's, that of double negation. It might seem that we intuitively perceive the truth of the proposition '*p* is equivalent to not not-*p*'. Certainly in most natural languages double negation is equivalent to affirmation. In some (as in Cockney and sometimes in Shakespeare's) it functions only as a strengthened negation. Now we may suppose a more primitive language from which both these latter kinds develop which contains the expression 'not-*p*'. Using this simple language, all speakers may communicate without difficulty; and it would be strange to say that they must really already mean something different by 'not-*p*' because later they will differ in the usage of the further expression, which has not yet emerged, 'not not-*p*'. When one of them says, 'That is not green', and another agrees, we should hardly say that they were making different statements—if they are both looking at the same thing and using their eyes—whatever development were subsequently to follow.

Undoubtedly certain ways of developing an existing system seem natural to us, and others unnatural; and mathematical systems and developments of such systems also prove useful. We can apply them in engineering or economics. But that such a system is useful must remain an empirical matter; a system that has no useful application does not cease to be a system on that account. One may build a structure with wires, and afterwards, perhaps, make use of it as a plate-stand; or one may exhibit it at the Tate Gallery and call it 'St. John the Baptist'. But its success or failure in either of these roles does not affect its character merely as a structure of wires. Mathematics may be studied either for the sake of its beauty or its utility; but the establishing of such claims with reference to any given calculus or technique is not itself a mathematical undertaking.

Wittgenstein's treatment of Mathematics, I have claimed, throws light on his conception of natural languages. 'To invent a language', he says, 'could mean to invent an instrument for a particular purpose on the basis of the laws of nature (or consistently with them).'[1] Here we see the same sort of notions at work. And indeed it is to illustrate his general view of languages that he introduces his example of the continuation of mathematical series. He imagines a case such as that of someone who, told to continue the series '200, 202, 204 . . .' goes on from three hundred, '303, 306, 309 . . .' and from four hundred, '404, 408, 412 . . .' We might attempt, in face of this unexpected response, to get this person to see it as we do; but it always remains possible that we shall fail. 'You were told', we may say, 'to go on in the *same* way.' But perhaps he will answer that that is just what he has done. A different analogy has struck him; he finds it natural to call a different kind of development 'the same'. At a certain point we will give up. We can give people reasons for doing a thing in one way rather than another, so long as their ultimate proclivities are the same as our own; but the process must come to an end. And if, this end being reached, we still differ, then there can be no more that we can do.

And so too when we are challenged to justify any of our ordinary beliefs; we give reasons, but when we have given all the reasons we can—have made all the possible moves within the language-game as we play it—there is no more we can offer. There comes a point, Wittgenstein writes, where he is inclined to say, 'This is simply what I do.'[2] We can imagine beings to whom it is natural to behave differently, but beyond a certain point it will be impossible to converse or dispute with them.

---

[1] *PI*, 492. He adds that the phrase has also another sense, analogous to that in which we speak of the invention of a game.

[2] *PI*, 217.

'So you are saying that human agreement decides what is true and false.' These words Wittgenstein puts in to the mouth of an imaginary critic—that victim of philosophical puzzlement whom he eternally wrestles with—and answers: 'It is what human beings *say* that is true or false; and they agree in the language they use. That agreement is not in opinions but in forms of life.'[1]

Our linguistic activities are part of that pattern of things that makes us what we are and determines our relationships with our fellows. That men have, within limits, similar basic proclivities, that certain patterns of behaviour come naturally to almost all of them, is the condition of the emergence of society and language. It is within that general framework that particular linguistic activities go forward. We do not make things true or false by agreement. It is of particular statements that truth and falsehood are predicted; but it is clear that unless we agreed, not as to particular beliefs but in some fundamental mental orientation, the language in which the terms 'true' and 'false' occur could never have existed at all.

It is a different thing, therefore, to challenge a particular belief, for which reasons can be given, and to challenge a practice of the kind that defines the whole system, the pattern of activities itself. The giving of reasons, Wittgenstein says, must come to an end.

What for logical purposes is essentially the same point was long ago made in connexion with the foundation of morals. Sidgwick observes that one cannot proceed in any discussion of morals without the initial assumption that rational procedures for settling moral issues exist. 'Men never ask', he wrote, '"Why should I believe what I see to be true?" but they frequently ask, "Why should I do what I see to be right?" It

[1] *PI*, 241.

is easy to reply that the question is futile . . .'[1] Its futility was insisted on more strongly somewhat later by Pritchard. What is characteristic of Wittgenstein's handling of this type of argument is his use of the notion of a language-game, and his distinction between questions that fall within some particular game and those that seek to pass wholly beyond it. His characteristic approach emerges in the assertion that the latter must, if anything, be grammatical.

A philosophical dispute between say, a materialist and an idealist as to the reality of matter cannot be the same in kind as a non-philosophical dispute in the same idiom—a dispute say, as to whether some supposed particular object is real or mythical. Certain procedures are provided for the conduct of disputes of this latter kind within the system of existing linguistic practice. These language-forms have their significance in that setting. The metaphysical discussion, while ostensibly employing the same forms, in fact cuts them off from their context; it fails, therefore, to speak of what it intends to speak of. Rather it raises a grammatical question, for it calls in question a whole system of linguistic usage. We are asked say, whether a particular planet or a particular kind of chemical substance really exists; and these questions, as we have seen, can in principle be settled within the terms of existing language, within the rules of the game. But what of the question, 'Is matter real?' Indeed it is not hard to establish that matter is real if all that is called for is to show that some particular material thing—one's own hand, for instance—is real. The appropriate procedures are hardly esoteric. And an idealist who rejects such a demonstration must therefore be rejecting these procedures themselves. The denial of the reality of matter

[1] *Methods of Ethics*, seventh edition, p. 5. He goes on to observe that the demonstration of the futility of the question is not in fact wholly satisfactory by itself; for we still need some explanation of its persistency.

succeeds in asserting nothing about the world, but, if anything, disputes the legitimacy of a given language-game. And this game is one that in fact is played among men. There seems to be no further answer one can give than to say that.[1]

That it is played is no more than a matter of fact; it is always conceivable that it should not have been played. It might be said that the question raised is as to whether it ought to be played; and this formulation—one that Wittgenstein does not discuss—comes nearer, I believe, to the heart of the matter. But we have found that, if we seek to go beyond all existing rules, then on Wittgenstein's account, no questions of legitimacy can sensibly be raised. For the rest, it is true that if no one has ever used such a language, it never could have been said that the earth is round or the cat is on the mat. But here a hypothetical proposition suffices us. Life might never have emerged on earth, and it would have been no less true that the earth is a roughly spherical body of such and such a diameter. To say this, on the present hypothesis, is to say that if anyone were to play the material-object language-game, this proposition, given appropriate observations, is one that the rules would legitimate.

Our grammar determines the structure of our world; it tells us 'what kind of object anything is'.[2] Our language is integrated into a way of life, and is bound up with the most basic pattern of our daily behaviour. The place we assign ourselves in the world, the terms in which we see it, are reflected throughout our linguistic practices. We behave, for instance, in one way towards persons and in another towards things. We regard them and look at them differently. Certain philosophical systems seem to call the distinction in question—and we find ourselves looking strangely at the world. These are, Wittgenstein

[1] Cf. *PI*, 398.   [2] *PI*, 373.

says, deep disorders; these doubts philosophy raises concern the whole structure of our attitudes.

A difference in attitude, on Wittgenstein's view, is to be distinguished from a difference in belief. Philosophers often seek grounds for what they call our belief in other people's minds; but Wittgenstein denies that this is a belief.[1] To treat a person as a person is to adopt an attitude to him: a kind of attitude that we do not adopt otherwise—except perhaps, half in earnest, though half instinctively, to pictures of people and the like; children may adopt it to dolls. Our attitudes appear in the ways in which we behave and look. Suppose that we came among some strange race of beings, and presently came to be convinced that we were dealing not with people but with automata—or that we thought that of our present associates. It would be this, our attitudes, not our beliefs that would have to change. These notions form a logically connected set in Wittgenstein's terminology—forms of life, attitudes and grammar. Our attitudes are embodied in our language and expressed in its grammar. Together they define the limits of discourse— limits beyond which we cannot pass. What has to be accepted, he says, is a form of life.[2]

In general I have reserved criticism of Wittgenstein for a separate chapter to follow when the present task, that of achieving some tolerably adequate view of his position, shall be complete. Nonetheless I prefer not to pass on from the point which we have reached without some words of comment. The doctrines we have been examining are integral in Wittgenstein's thought and it will be well to state at once the main objections that they are exposed to.

Broadly the thesis is that a language, like a mathematical system, consists of a complex set of procedures, which may also

[1] Cf. *PI*, p. 178.   [2] *PI*, p. 226.

be appealed to as rules. Normative notions—rightness, validity, and we may perhaps add truth—are significant inasmuch as there exist standards which we can appeal to and principles we can invoke. But where a new move is first made, a new development takes place, clearly no such standard can be applicable; we have moved beyond existing practice. Wittgenstein, it seems, is committed to holding that no such step can be called right or wrong; no evaluative assessment is possible. At most we can predict, as a practical matter, that its adoption will prove useful or otherwise.

Now, if so, it will be well to appreciate for a start the violence done here to our ordinary linguistic usage. It is clear that mathematicians working beyond, no less than within, the present body of Mathematics believe that there are right answers to be found. Wittgenstein's account might perhaps be strengthened if he distinguished between rightness and goodness. A move within a given system might then be called right or wrong by appeal to existing rules; but a proposed new extension of the system—or, if we can put ourselves outside them, the various systems themselves—could only be recommended or condemned as good or bad.[1] It will remain true, even so, that in calling any new procedure good we shall have no standard to appeal to; to call it so will be no more than an

[1] The distinction is made with great force by Professor J. N. Findlay in his British Academy Lecture for 1957, 'The Structure of the Kingdom of Ends' (at the time of writing still unpublished). It may perhaps be maintained that Wittgenstein's intention is not to deny that such new moves as we have spoken of, in Mathematics or elsewhere, can properly be called right or wrong, but only to reject a particular mistaken picture, that of correspondence or non-correspondence with a realm of mathematical fact; they are not right or wrong as a copy is right or wrong. But how, on such a view, can Mathematics be said to 'create norms'? Clearly there can be no right or wrong before the norms are created. And again, why should Wittgenstein have taken Ramsey's remark that Logic is a normative science as implying a comparison to a calculus with exact rules, if assertions of this sort can be made where no such appeal is in question?

act of legislation—a decision, as Wittgenstein says. And here we are still at variance with usage; for we are normally said to realize, to come to see or appreciate—not to lay it down at will —that this or that course is good or bad.

Now doubtless it may be legitimate to diverge from current linguistic practice when occasion demands it; ordinary language has no sacrosanctity. The *status quo* may be allowed a certain initial claim; but where good reasons can be shown for introducing changes, even for developing different modes of speaking for specifically philosophical purposes, we should be clearly wrong not to do so. Wittgenstein's position here, however, is weaker than that of other philosophers. For one thing he has explicitly laid it down that our ordinary expressions are 'in order as they are', and has forbidden philosophers to tamper with them.[1] But the difficulty goes deeper. His own system makes no provision for the adoption of any new way of speaking in conflict with existing practice. If we refer to the rules of the present language-game it will simply be counted as wrong; otherwise we must think of it as belonging to another language-game of its own. And we have seen that it is a large part of Wittgenstein's thesis that between the practititioners of two such ultimately different sets of linguistic practices, no argument is possible.

Now he is committed, it seems, to withholding the predicates 'right' and 'wrong' in certain contexts where ordinary usage applies them. His own procedure, then, is exposed to the general dilemma we have stated: either this new usage is in itself wrong, as it must be if our appeal is to existing practice; or else what he uses here is a different language, and we cannot talk with him. In neither case can he give logically cogent reasons for his innovations.

Let us look again at the doctrine. Our linguistic practices

[1] *PI*, 98 and 124.

reflect our nature—what we are. And when we arrive at ultimate practices no further discussion is possible. We can conceive creatures differently constituted, but we could not dispute
with them. Disputation is possible within a system, between
beings who share practices which they can appeal to; these
practices have also the force of rules. One might say, in the
language of our eighteenth-century moral philosophers, that
what Wittgenstein calls grammar belongs to or reflects our
arbitrary constitution. Where constitutions differ there is no
appeal. Thus to us it is natural, in Wittgenstein's example, to
continue the series he sets out in one particular way; we can
imagine beings whose natural proclivities are different; but, to
repeat, discourse with them would be impossible.

Wittgenstein gives numerous examples of curious language-
games. He imagines, too, that someone given the series,
'2, 4, 6, 8 . . .' and told to continue it in the same way, goes
on as we should until he get to 1000, and then proceeds,
'1004, 1008, 1012 . . .' and so on. Yet so long as there is some
method, some pattern, we shall still say that these are languages, though strange ones. Here various considerations suggest
themselves. It seems that in some sense the language presupposes the pattern. And the patterns are really there to be seen.
Wittgenstein says that we make certain practices into rules; he
does not go so far as to say that we make them patterns. It may
be worth remarking, too, that some patterns are more truly
patterns than others, they have, we may say, a better *Gestalt*.
And that, too, is not of our making.

The other line of thought that Wittgenstein's examples suggest to me is this. The alternative continuation of the series,
though strange to us, is not wholly unintelligible. A single
system, then, if it is a flexible one, may find room for the
recognition of different patterns which may or may not com-
pete. Where they do—and it is these cases we are concerned

with—then no doubt different people will proceed differently. But where we differ we also seek agreement. Wittgenstein seems to contemplate no mean between creatures whose proclivities are identical in these cases, and creatures whose proclivities are incommensurable. Either we appeal to the existing rules and agreement is possible, or else we each play our own games and there is no room for argument. But the truth is that our proclivities partly diverge and partly coincide. Where they diverge understanding need not break down; it is possible to see more patterns than one; Wittgenstein's own examples teach us that. The possibility of argument and reasoning no less than the need for it arise from this, that we naturally follow partly divergent courses, and also naturally seek to assimilate them; for a background of understanding remains.

The essence of rational discourse is the search for agreement. Wittgenstein's failure to take account of it, I suggest, prejudices his whole picture of language. Indeed he sees agreement in certain fundamental tendencies—existing conformity —as the basis of discourse, without which it would be impossible; but he fails to see it as an end, as something dynamic. It is what we may call the postulate of rationality that ideally agreement is possible.

Clearly to call a statement rational is not to assert that all men ever will, or even might, agree about it; for some are always too stupid or too prejudiced. It is to assert, we may tautologously say, that all men would agree, supposing they were rational. The tautological formulation has this use, that it brings home to us the typical application of the postulate, namely in situations where different procedures seem natural to different people. That there are conclusions to be reached, which are also those that ought to be reached—this, not merely existing conformity, is what is presupposed in the possibility of discourse.

A language, we are told, is a form of life. Human nature is reflected in human grammar—in our ultimate linguistic prac- tices. Human beings, then, naturally adopt divergent or partly divergent linguistic practices—and they naturally seek to assi- milate them. Assimilation might be most quickly achieved by the use of indoctrination or drugs. But what is presupposed in what—in Wittgenstein's terminology—we shall call an attitude, namely, the attitude of rationality, must be something more than that. It involves the adoption of procedures of certain kinds; it assumes that out of the search for agreement, through not drugs but argument and criticism, right answers and not wrong ones will tend to come. I deliberately use normative words for I do not think the attitude in question, whether it is commendable or otherwise, can fairly be described without them. And the attitude certainly exists; it, like others, gener- ates forms of language and systems of procedures. If existing practice or natural bent is to be appealed to, this attitude, these procedures and tendencies have as good a right to be recog- nized as any other. Yet its acceptance seems to be incompatible with the account of logic we have been looking at in the present chapter. It is incompatible with the view that where no stan- dard practices can be referred to, no normative judgements can apply; that here all courses are open, all alike are beyond good and evil. They need not be so; we may have a practice of seek- ing rational agreement even there.

I may perhaps be told that in all this I have been taking too literally what Wittgenstein says of standards or rules. Thus in the case of a mathematician who has found some new proof, Wittgenstein, it may be said, means to assert neither that it would be grammatically correct to describe him as having reached a decision—a decision to use a certain rule—nor yet that that would be a superior usage, or one that we ought generally to adopt. 'Why should we not say', he asks, 'that in a proof we have won through to a decision?'[1] He offers this as no more than a new way of looking at that kind of activity; it is a suggested point of view, not a theory. In this account of Wittgenstein's purpose there would be much truth, certainly. He says in effect, 'Try thinking of the thing as a decision',— so as to help us to see it for what it is. Yet in the end the dilemma still faces us. Where there are no rules to appeal to we can only decide; and I suppose that it is primarily on this account that the step is called a decision. The situation, it seems, is simply this. We suppose that certain steps go beyond existing practice: if it is true that such steps are inevaluable, are neither right nor wrong, we do not need to speak in pictures or riddling analogies but can plainly assert the fact; but if it is false the analogy is then useless, for then evaluation here will no longer be analogous to any appeal to existing rules.

Let us suppose that Wittgenstein gives us only a kind of picture or model of language—a dualistic model. We are to think of two factors in language; on the one hand particular moves or practices which are assessed by appeal to the rules, and on the other hand those rules themselves. Beyond these there is no further appeal; they are things we merely accept or adopt. Such a model, it may be claimed, serves to bring out, by its artificially sharp dichotomy, a distinction that is obscured in the shifting complexities of actual language; it helps us to see our way through; and yet in this we may have no more than a model. I shall suggest, however, that it is a model in which certain views or assumptions are embodied, and others excluded. We must not assume, for instance, that our language as it stands is necessarily even self-consistent. Suppose it is not. Then, perhaps, we shall alter one procedure on appeal to another, the second on appeal to a third, and we may finally alter the third on appeal to the first in its altered form; and

[1] *RFM*, ii, 27.

none of these is in practice taken as ultimate. But here deeper doubts surely suggest themselves: we may ask whether the model we used, even though we regard it as no more, does not obscure more than it clarifies. I should claim in fact that what we have here are two radically different views of language; and the conflict between them is not removed by calling one or the other a mere picture. In the one the key notion is that of a rule: practices are appealed to as standards. Hence a new practice there, or an extension of the rules, can only be adopted by decision; it is something that falls outside the ordinary operation of language. In the other view all this appears differently. Here the emergence of new forms, and the processes whereby they emerge—forms of thought or of language, the two determine each other—is seen as part of the essence of the system. The whole dichotomy is thus called in question; and the body of thought generally is not treated as a game with given rules, but as a developing and self-corrective system or organism. We no longer need to invoke some particular new procedure, decision, to account for the possibility of such developments: they are an integral part of its working.

We may speak more generally indeed, for this notion of a decision is the *passe-partout* of contemporary philosophy; we meet it everywhere, in logic and mathematics and morals. What gap is it, one might ask, that this great makeshift is called in to fill? The notion that these philosophers apparently find unintelligible is a very simple one, that of novelty, of the discovery of new truths by reason; that is why we come on 'decisions' at every turn.

III

Inner Experience

Hitherto we have examined the application of Wittgenstein's linguistic method only to problems connected with language itself, or to closely kindred problems of logic. One of the themes of *Philosophical Investigations*, around which much discussion revolves, is the status of the concept of experience, and of the privacy that we attribute to experience. Here we are on old philosophical ground; we are in the midst of that dark forest of problems in which, straying from the path, Modern Philosophy has got lost. For, to Wittgenstein, the form of any philosophical problem may be expressed by the words, 'I do not know my way about.'[1] These issues, then, are the natural ones to take if we are to see the application of the method in a further and rather fuller sample.

The philosophical position Wittgenstein is seeking to break down might be roughly identified as Dualism; though at the risk of leaving the impression that he proposes to replace it by something that would be called Monism. But Monism, mentalistic or materialist, is for Wittgenstein only another, deeper error. Realizing the untenability of Dualism, philosophers who are too far in to turn back seek to find a secure bottom still deeper. But for the present our concern is with Dualism.

With the outer world, it seems, we are all familiar. Here there are things which we can see and know; there is a knowing subject and known objects, which exist independently of one another—objects such that they can be mistaken and must be

[1] Cf. *PI*, 123.

identified, but which, presented squarely before us, we can normally recognize. All men are inhabitants of this public world; but each is supposed by the dualist to live also in an inner world of his own. Here too there are objects, but objects which only he can see and know.

Those outer objects that we look at and recognize we can also mistake; but these, merely by looking at them, we necessarily know for what they are. Each person perceives directly the contents of his own mind, his private realm; but from other people's he is necessarily excluded. What a man experiences he knows, and cannot help but know; but what others experience, he must infer from what he finds in the outer world. On this view spirit and matter—or else perhaps, experience and matter—are two distinct kinds of substance, of existent thing; it is a fact that they are very closely related, but it would seem to be theoretically possible that they might have been related differently, or not at all.

Now, what it is like to hope or fear, to feel pain, to think of this or that, most of us are familiar with. The doctrine before us, then, tells us nothing that we are ignorant of as to our experience of our inner life. Rather it presents it in pictorial form; we are to discuss the application of a picture. But even that, we shall have to add, portrays less inner experience itself, than the linguistic forms we employ when we speak of it. And it portrays it badly.

Dualists have intended to characterize a class of objects or a realm of being. It is Wittgenstein's thesis that such intended philosophical descriptions of the world break down, and prove to be no more than accounts of grammar. We must recall the distinction between questions falling within a given language-game, and those structural questions that seek rather to comprehend the game as a whole, or to go beyond it. If we are to discuss the contents of the world we must use the language-forms belonging to such discussion; but these yield only ordinary scientific or particular factual questions. If we are to go beyond that, then, in effect, we can do no more than set forth or represent these forms say, in a pictorial way—or else misrepresent them, confusing them with others. Indeed it is Wittgenstein's general thesis that philosophical perplexities arise when, deceived by similarities of form and neglectful of differences of function, we interpret one part of our linguistic system on the false analogy of some other. The dualist picture of the mind which we have been sketching derives from our interpreting the language of experience in terms of the language of public objects; for the private realm we spoke of is an attempt to see mental life in the image of the world of common things. We ordinarily speak of people as perceiving physical things, tables and chairs and the like; the dualist speaks of the mind as perceiving inward entities, ideas, images or acts of will. He reads the one language-game in terms of the other. But it seems further that two separate mistakes must be involved, though some difficulties remain as to their relation to one another.[1] First, we suppose ourselves to be dealing with two ontological realms, when we are in fact dealing with two parts of language; secondly we misinterpret the one, the language-game of inward experience, and force on it the grammar of the language-game of the public world of things. The language in which we speak of private experience is in fact part of a larger, public language, and is learnt in social contexts. We learn the meaning of such words as 'pain' when people get hurt, are consoled, attended to, and so on. And having before merely cried out, we too first learn to complain and seek help. The language is given meaning in its context, and without it would have none; hence the possible expression of pain is involved in the concept in a way that has no parallel in our

[1] See below, pp. 193–5.

concepts of physical things. But this may appear more plainly presently.

The dualist conceives us as learning these concepts not in any social context, but privately, from our own experience. It follows from the picture he draws that one might live and move wholly in one's own private world; philosophers have often thought of this as our starting point, from which we progress to the discovery of outer things. And indeed it has puzzled them how in the circumstances we are able to make that discovery at any stage; and still more, how we penetrate the private world of any other person. This doctrine supposes the possibility of a private language—a language that will permit references to nothing but the speaker's own experiences—if only that it may be expressible. Indeed the error Wittgenstein finds will apparently cut both ways. It is as a result of misreading the language of experience in terms of the language of public objects that the dualist is led to see the mind as its own place, a world to itself. But that picture in turn requires that each mind may possess its own language, functioning, as it was learnt, wholly inwardly. Such a language will be necessarily private. For other people have no direct access to these experiences, and can only infer their existence from public objects that they observe; but those cannot be mentioned in this language. The notion may be thought to give no difficulty. It seems that we often talk to ourselves in an inner monologue; yet in that monologue we still refer to things that are in 'the outside world', and we speak a language that we have learnt from other people. We are to suppose a language derived from and confined to the sphere of our inward experience.[1] Wittgenstein denies that such a language is possible.

Such an imaginary private language will not correspond to the language of experience as it exists as part of ordinary

[1] Cf. *PI*, 244.

speech. Here the inner and outer, we may say, are halves of a single whole; but if we break up the ordinary language-game, if we take the two halves in isolation, then each must become a whole in itself. Then, interpreting our linguistic discussion as a discussion about existent things, we are left with the mutual exclusion of two separate and self-contained worlds.

Such is the dualist picture, but it is unworkable; and struggling to free ourselves, we are only the more entangled. Dualism leads on to Behaviourism. For we have been told to think of a man's inner experience, his mental images, his feelings and the like, as forming a class of objects which lie hidden from the rest of us in some closed place; they are objects which only he can perceive. The rest of us may observe how he speaks and behaves, and how he reacts to our behaviour and speech, but not the springs that impel this visible performance; these we can only reach by inference. If so they play no part in our lives; if his outward behaviour meets all our ordinary needs, and is all, so to speak, that we shall ever treat with, then the inward object drops out of consideration as irrelevant. It seems not to matter whether or not those inward objects are there in their secret lockers, so long as anything that we can hope to see or know will be the same. The behaviourist, therefore, rejects them as a fiction; and indeed a fiction would serve as well as an entity of which we can know nothing.[1]

Yet Wittgenstein himself has been thought a behaviourist. For, one asks, if Dualism is rejected—and though the term is not used, the standpoint is clear enough—what other alternative remains? But Wittgenstein does not mean to offer any alternative, any other or newer theory or picture. It suffices that the ordinary forms of discourse concerning experience exist and function satisfactorily. Here as elsewhere what we require is to observe, to note, not to explain, the practice of a

[1] *PI*, 293; cf. 304.

particular language-game. Dualism in fact tells us nothing; all we need here is to let go of a picture. The task Wittgenstein sets himself is a negative one; the old picture is not to be replaced by any other. Yet that dualist picture is one that forces itself on us so strongly that it seems that if we reject Behaviourism we leave no other possibility to turn to. Indeed the impression that Wittgenstein's work has created may arise from other factors too: for there are, certainly, forms of mentalism that he opposes. We have seen above how we fall into a wrong view of understanding: failing to recognize that to understand a word is, generally speaking, to know how to use it, and realizing that it must be more than the possession of any sort of feelings and images, philosophers are apt to think of it as some yet more ethereal process; the purely mental act occurs in some finer, gaseous medium. Wittgenstein denies this, and because he denies it, he says, he will be thought to be rejecting mental processes generally.[1]

We must see first that no matter of fact is at issue; there is no question of the existence or non-existence of a class of objects. Our only concern is with the appropriateness of a mode of pictorial representation. The rejection of behaviourism, Wittgenstein says—the denial that pain is a form of behaviour—may have an air of obscurantism; but only because the grammatical discussion is mistaken for an ontological one.[2]

Our concern is with language, not reality. In some sense experience is clearly private; one person cannot be said literally to feel another's feelings. To say that is to notice a point

---

[1] *PI*, 308. Cf. above, pp. 24–5. It may perhaps be worth adding the suggestion that much of the perplexity of Professor Ryle's *Concept of Mind* arises from the confusion of something like this relatively modest and certainly plausible thesis with some other far wider but also far less defensible one. For to say this, and no more than this, is not to get rid of Dualism or 'privileged access' or the problem of our knowledge of other people's minds.

[2] *RFM*, ii, 79.

in grammar; and we might teach the use of the word in this way, by saying 'Experience is private.' It would be like saying that a rod necessarily has a certain length, or that colours are visible.[1] These terms 'physical object' and 'experience' are grammatically different.[2] And this difference requires to be stressed, for the dualist error is to assimilate them. Grammar allows us to say that two people see the same table; it forbids us to say that two people have felt the same pain. Again it forbids us, in the case of mathematical entities, say of numbers, to talk of our seeing or feeling them at all. Numbers are not invisible objects as some perfectly transparent stuff might be invisible; for the notion of seeing them is absurd. That is the kind of difference we are concerned with.

Supposing that a man reports that he is in pain, there can be no question of his being in error; he may be lying, but that is a different matter. This infallibility is quite unlike that which attaches to the most reliable statements about physical objects. Suppose that an object is before one's eyes; one looks at it and says what it is. No doubt a report given in these circumstances can normally be relied on. But the object has still to be identified, its typical features can be pointed out; and it still could quite intelligibly be said that it had been identified wrongly. But the report that one is in pain is, in this respect, more like a cry, an exclamation; there can be no question of right and wrong here, there is no place for doubt.[3] One is tempted to say that a person in pain must also know that he is in pain. Now he certainly feels it—that is part of the meaning of 'pain'. The feeling comes, and one reports it; but there is nothing more. It is true that it makes no sense to say that a man mistakenly believes himself to be in pain; if to claim that he knows it is no more than a way of saying that, then Wittgenstein would not have disputed it.

[1] Cf. *PI*, 251–3; cf. 295.   [2] Cf. *PI*, 293.   [3] Cf. *PI*, 244.

Wittgenstein speaks of a philosophical discussion in the course of which one of the disputants was moved to strike his breast and cry, 'But surely only I can have *this* pain!'[1] In so doing, Wittgenstein says, he was testifying in a dramatic way to his adherence to existing grammatical practice. Such sentences as 'I felt *his* twinge of pain' are allotted no ordinary function, and that state of affairs is represented by the dualist in the form of a picture. We feel it natural to say, first, that one cannot feel another man's pain, and then to interpret the statement on the analogy of others, such as that one cannot, in a given case, open another man's strong-box. No enlightenment comes of insisting, with whatever conviction, that these are indeed the linguistic practices we follow; that is not in doubt. The poet Collins wrote,

> Smite thy bosom sage, and tell
> What is truth and which the way?

'Why smite his bosom?' Boswell asked. 'Why, Sir,' said Johnson, 'to show he was in earnest.'

Our ability to form a picture signifies nothing; our inability signifies no more. It is the application of the picture that concerns us. We tend to think of blindness as a kind of cloud, a darkness in the head of the blind man; but when we reflect on the picture and see that it has no use, no application, we do not seek to replace it by another.[2] What we cannot imagine we dismiss as impossible; what we cling to, our images and pictures, are often idle and inapplicable.[3] When someone asserts that only he can experience his own pain, Wittgenstein asks whom he is telling that, and to what end. The assertion belongs to no language-game; it makes no connexion with the rest of our usage. Differently put, certainly, it might serve as an

[1] Cf. *PI*, 253.   [2] *PI*, 424.   [3] Cf. *PI*, 395-7.

unexceptionable grammatical proposition, such as that colours are visible.

What we require is to get a clear view of the language-game in which in fact talk of experience operates. The dualist thinks of two things which he sees as connected: a physical object, namely a human body, and an experience say, of pain, which occurs when that object is, for instance, heated or kicked. No reason appears in logic why it should not be with objects of any other sort, say with a block of wood or a frying-pan, that the pain is associated. Its lacking the means of expressing it, and our consequent ignorance, would be an empirical matter. Yet clearly this is to do violence to the grammar of our terms; we speak, not of objects, but of persons as having experiences. A person may have a pain in the hand, and in a sense the pain may be said to be associated with the hand. Yet it is he, not the hand, that complains; and it is to him, not to his hand, that we express our sympathy. To be sure, a mother might say, 'Poor little hand' if it got hurt, and kiss it better; but that is half playful. Even if we regularly behaved like that it would not serve the dualist's case; for then it can only be said, in so far as the situation is sanely conceivable at all, that we should be treating hands as people, or as if they were people. A frying-pan, Wittgenstein remarks, might indeed get hurt in a fairy story; but there it can also complain.[1]

To regard someone as a person is to adopt an attitude towards him. Only to persons, and what resembles them—to animals in some measure, and in make-believe perhaps to dolls —can one express pity, encouragement or spite. To kick the stone one has stumbled on is to make a mistake in logical grammar. Something of the way in which the parts of the language-game fit together appears if we try to imagine a stone or a block of wood in acute pain. One might as well imagine

[1] Cf. *PI*, 282 ff.

the number seven in pain. Let it only be a fly, Wittgenstein says, something that can wriggle, and the notion of pain begins to make sense again; here it can get some sort of foothold.[1] These linguistic usages are built around certain types of situation; one cannot remove the central block and leave the structure that rests on it standing. It is from the human body that we take our prototype or paradigm of consciousness.[2] To seek to do without it, yet to play the language-game which revolves round it, is like worshipping without a God, or fighting without an enemy—both things, we may note, which in a shadowy way people suppose themselves to do. It is again somewhat as if we were to form our notion of Metaphysical Poetry say, from the practice of Donne and Cowley, and then to ask whether Donne and Cowley themselves were truly metaphysical poets. Words like 'pain' are given their meaning, we have seen, in social contexts in which the expression of pain plays a part. Isolate them from these contexts, as the dualist does, and their ordinary use and meaning is destroyed. But the error appears in this, that if the grammar of sensations is read in terms of that of physical objects, one would then clearly need to identify one's own pain, as one does one's own fountain-pen; and one always might conceivably be mistaken.[3]

But with these considerations we are led back to the crucial and central issue of privacy. Surely, it will be said, a person's

[1] *PI*, 284; cf. 282 and 310.

[2] This point is brought out very clearly by Professor Malcolm in his valuable review of *Philosophical Investigations* in *The Philosophical Review*, lxiii, No. 4, pp. 530-2, which I have also made use of elsewhere.

[3] 'That expression of doubt has no place in the language-game; but if we cut out human behaviour, which is the expression of sensation, it looks as if I might begin *legitimately* to doubt afresh. My temptation to say that one might take a sensation for something other than what it is arises from this: if I assume the abrogation of the normal language-game with the expression of the sensation, I need a criterion for the identity for the sensation; and then the possibility of error also exists.' (*PI*, 288.)

paradigm of consciousness is his own experience. One knows from one's own case what it is to feel pain; that is something that we are acquainted with directly. Other people's we arrive at by inference; and their behaviour, the expression of pain, is then no more than the evidence or data that we use. It becomes clear how in the last resort everything turns on the possibility of a private language; for here, of course, we have the dualist picture we started with. To say that we have an inward paradigm, for instance, of pain, is to say that one might tell oneself what pain is, or record at any moment that one is in pain, without ever passing beyond that circle of our own experience or learning the common language of other men.

That picture, once again, shows us our inner life as a private realm of objects that reduplicates the realm of everyday. In Locke, for instance, the metaphor is explicit; reflection is compared to an inward eye that is turned upon the contents of the mind. To know what pain is, therefore, one needs only look inward to one's own experience; so long as one knows this, which is what the word stands for, then one has its whole use in a nutshell.[1] But it will not only be of such words as 'pain' that we must say that; the mind contains visual images and sensations as well as feelings. In one's own mind one has one's own specimens that give one the meaning of 'red' and 'hard' and 'angular' no less than of 'pain', and it is these that one originally has knowledge of. It follows that when two people speak of a red apple, no less than when they speak of an acute pain, they cannot really be speaking of the same thing, or even in the same language. Each has his own exemplar, his own sensation, from which his word 'red' takes its meaning; each is debarred from the sight of his neighbour's. The two can never be compared. But if some one uses the word 'pain' and so doing, speaks to and communicates with other people, it

[1] Cf. *PI*, 264.

must be the ordinary word, with its public meaning, not the word we gave meaning to by a private reference, that he uses.[1] If we still cling to the dualist picture, and, allowing a public meaning to the word 'pain', yet claim that there is something, even if its nature is inexpressible, that remains behind, we shall still find that the words we are using, so long as we use any at all—here the word 'something'—belong to public speech.

In all this the privacy of sensations is not in doubt; for that is a part of the language-game. 'Sensations are private', I have said, is for Wittgenstein a grammatical proposition that we might use in teaching the word. Only one who feels pain can report it, and if he sincerely says that he is in pain he cannot be wrong. Somewhat similarly, someone who has learnt the five-times table can repeat it; but we have seen that in order to repeat it correctly, it is not necessary that he should be at the same time glancing or gazing mentally at a private image. He does not look inward and proceed accordingly. These two cases, that of reporting one's feelings and that of repeating what one has learnt, are very different in other ways; but in both what must be rejected is the notion that a correct report or performance can only follow on an act of inward inspection. We must put away the picture of a man who, having looked into a secret box, is reliably informed of its contents; who knows because he has seen.

Ostensive definition is also a performance that has a function in the public world; and here the exhibition of a single sample may serve to give meaning to a word. It establishes criteria of identification. There are certain procedures of showing or pointing, and rules for the subsequent linguistic conduct of those who assist at them. If words are to be given meaning in a private language, a private ostensive definition will be neces-sary. Let us suppose that one is to give a name to a certain

[1] Cf. *PI*, 272-4.

sensation.[1] Perhaps one concentrates one's attention on one's own experience; as it were, one points inwardly. Wittgenstein asks what purpose this private ceremony serves—for it seems to be a ceremony and no more. Perhaps it has the effect of impressing on one's own mind at once the sensation and its name, so as to ensure the future right use of the latter. Indeed so long as we have a public system of reference by which to judge of right and wrong such an act of self-impression might so serve. But in a necessarily private language no means of determining right and wrong can exist.

Here we have the crux of Wittgenstein's argument. To speak a language, on his view, is to take part in a certain form of social activity which, moreover, is governed by rules. Hence conduct may be condemned as wrong or irregular; the procedures of an individual may diverge from accepted procedures. We have a standard to which to refer it. In the case of a private language no such appeal can be possible; there can be no such thing as divergent or irregular practice, and hence the notion of such a language is nonsensical.[2]

It may be said, perhaps, that a man's practice at one time may conflict with his practice at another, even though there is no further appeal. Let us suppose that at a given time a certain sensation occurs, and, by the kind of process we spoke of, one gives it a name. Later the same sensation recurs—or so one says. One repeats the name. Surely, it will be said, one can be right or wrong; one's present use of the name can be the same as or different from one's previous use of it. Certainly it may be so, provided that some possible reference beyond the speaker's own sensation exists. But failing that, we shall have to say that whatever he himself calls the same is so. For there is no other test. And then clearly the notion is nonsensical. It seems that we are apt to take for granted this concept of sameness,

[1] Cf. *PI*, 256 ff.   [2] Cf. *PI*, 199–202.

even when we are most critical of others; but it too must belong to a given language-game. We raised the question with reference to someone who, being told to continue the series, '200, 202, 204 . . .' proceeds after reaching three hundred, '303, 306, 309 . . .' It would be said that he is now proceeding differently —and in terms of our language-game we shall be right to say so. But according to his own private language, this way of continuing it may be called 'the same'. It seems there is no continuation that may not be called the same in some usage. The word 'same' itself is governed by rules that must be applied in any instance; and there is no kind of practice that may not be said, at least, *per impossibile*, in a private language, to be in accordance with some sort of rule.

We must repeat, then, that in a private language someone who calls one of his sensations the same as one that he has felt before cannot be in error; there is nothing from which his usage can diverge. It is true, of course, that speaking, as we do, a public language, we may check our memories one against another. But a possible appeal to a public standard is presupposed; there is always something our practice can conflict with. As to the notion of checking one impression by another in a private language, Wittgenstein compares that to buying a second copy of the morning paper to check the first.[1]

This argument has been criticized by Professor Ayer.[2] He paraphrases Wittgenstein as arguing that merely to check one sensation against another can never be enough, for if one cannot be trusted to recognize the one, one cannot be trusted to recognize another. He objects that unless there is something that one is allowed to recognize, no test can ever be completed.

[1] *PI*, 265.
[2] Can There be a Private Language? Symposium, *Aristotelian Society, Supplementary Volume*, xxviii (1954), p. 68. Cf. also *The Problem of Knowledge* (1956), pp. 63-4.

And then no use of words can be justified. Thus it will make no ultimate difference whether what one is to recognize, relying on one's own powers of recognition, is a sensation or a public object visible to everyone.

From a Wittgensteinian point of view, however, the two situations are very different. One may be said to recognize or to misrecognize an object before one; one's practice—the speaking of such and such words in face of this sort of object— either conforms or fails to conform to accepted practice. But in this sense there can be no question of the recognition of sensations—if to recognize a thing is to see it rightly. Here, once again, there is no seeing, no inward act of contemplation that grasps or fails to grasp an inward object. A feeling occurs, and one utters a certain sound. It may be said that one might utter a different sound from what one uttered when the same feeling occurred before, and in that sense recognize or misrecognize it. But that is a supposition we have already spoken of. Unless these words 'different' and 'same' belong to a public language, unless there is a usage against which ours is to be checked, there is no test of difference or sameness. Whatever we say here will be right—in the sense that there is nothing it can con- flict with. It could be said to conflict with our own previous practice, only if there were rules that could stand above both that practice and the present performance to which appeal might be made.

I do not intend to enter here into any extended criticism of Wittgenstein's treatment of inner experience. It will be seen that it is closely bound up with his general view of the status of rules in a language, and that was criticized in the previous chapter at some length. The two, it seems to me, must stand or fall together. If the notions of right and wrong cannot be adequately accounted for in terms of conformity to established practices or rules, then it would seem that it cannot be shown that within a wholly private system they are necessarily inapplicable. It is worth remarking that Wittgenstein allows it to be conceivable that we might discover that all mathematicians had been wrong on some point over the last thousand years, but apparently denies that it can sensibly be said that they may all always be wrong on any point.

It seems to me that our paradigm of sensations, for instance, of pain, is in some sense our own experience, and not what we observe of others; and further, that some sort of rudimentary language in which it might be spoken of, is after all conceivable. But this may be plainer when, in the next chapter, I come to speak of those aspects of language which Wittgenstein's treatment as it seems to me fails to take account of.

IV

Difficulties in Wittgenstein's Philosophy

I shall attempt no general assessment of Wittgenstein's achievement. Something of its scope and weight will have appeared in the previous chapters; and it is not my part to seek to place it, to supply a definite grading. It suffices that he has created a new way of philosophizing; and many contemporaries would assert further that since his work the old styles are obsolete. I cannot see Philosophy in this way; to me it is a subject where various large alternatives remain permanently open. I believe there will always be different forms of philosophy; but Wittgenstein has added to those possibilities. Another question for non-Wittgensteinians to ask will be how far these findings might fertilize other systems or be integrated with different modes of thought. This also I shall not attempt; I leave so vast an undertaking to others who may be equal to it. My aim in the present chapter is merely critical; I wish to set out as best I can the difficulties that stand in the way of accepting the Wittgensteinian position as I see it.

Wittgenstein disclaimed any intention of propounding a philosophy of language. To me it seems that he has done so whether he intended it or not. To tell us that languages resemble games; that the use of language is as much part of our natural history as eating or walking; that it is a particular form of public activity, interwoven with others and subject to rules; that language consists of an infinity of different parts, like so

many tools, each working in its own way, in its own context—
all this, I suggest, is to do as much in the way of a general
characterization as one could ask of any philosopher who had
made that his avowed object.[1] If so much is granted, a metaphysician will naturally wish to know why language should be
the only subject matter that lends itself to such treatment.
Surely there may be other fields of inquiry where no less
illumination may be got from a non-empirical, reflective
investigation. But that is a line of argument I shall not
pursue. My concern here is rather to ask whether the
present picture of language, upon which, for Wittgenstein,
everything turns, is not itself inadequate and vulnerable to
criticism.

Wittgenstein characterizes his own work as descriptive. He
explains nothing, he says, he merely lays before us the different
parts or segments of language, and points out the actual use of
different terms. He thus establishes for himself something like
a Socratic immunity from criticism; he professes to know
nothing—or nothing beyond what other people can see for
themselves. But the claim, or rather the disclaimer, may be
subject to suspicion in the one case no less than the other. What
Wittgenstein seems in fact to require of us, when he sets out
these things, is to understand the working of a mechanism; for
he tells us time and again to think of a word as a tool—there is
no saying of his that occurs more often. Wittgenstein's crucial
concept is of a language-game, a complex or system of linguistic activities; and every such game must be understood indivi-
dually, for each works to its own end and in its own particular
setting. Our endeavour in each case must be to see or grasp a
unique pattern, a system of relations; and language contains
at least as many such games as—to take not too remote an

---

[1] This question of the status we should attribute to Wittgenstein's pronounce-
ments on language was also discussed above. Cf. the note to p. 18.

analogy—there are concepts to be unfolded in the Hegelian Dialectic.

Now it seems that it would be possible to describe the action of a machine, to specify all its movements correctly, without understanding its working principle. And again one might describe all the procedures followed by the various players in a game without in any way appreciating the pattern. Yet that is what above all Wittgenstein requires us to appreciate. For consider the great purpose of all this—this descriptive setting-forth of language-games. It is to bring us to see that some particular move which we took for a move in the game has no proper place in it. Such a move is to be shown as failing to connect with the rest of the pattern. Wittgenstein compares it to a wheel spinning idly, disengaged from the machine it should belong to. Here we have a luminous metaphor—and yet no more than a metaphor. For there can be no way of testing whether this or that linguistic wheel has failed to engage, except to grasp the pattern in each case; to arrive at some sort of insight into that unique set of relations which it professes but fails to form a part of.

The point will bear repetition. We require an intuition into the unity of a complex, a grasp of the way in which a set of terms or elements cohere. If such old-fashioned language gives offence to contemporary ears, I regret it, but cannot retract it. Typical philosophical propositions, on Wittgenstein's view, lack integration with the rest; and clearly we must appreciate the pattern, the strength of the connexions where they hold, if we are also to see their failure where they fail. And yet it will certainly be possible to understand an accurate descriptive account, to agree on being shown, one after another, all the procedures involved in a given language-game, and yet fail to see that pattern, and hence also fail to see that want of connexion between a specified proposition and the rest. There would be no difficulty in finding children who would follow the one and fail to see the other—and, perhaps, no great difficulty in finding philosophers.

Supposing all this is granted, it is agreed that Wittgenstein in fact requires something more than a mere description, or the acceptance of a description, it may be asked what damaging consequences follow. It may be allowed, perhaps, that this ability to appreciate patterns is involved in the unravelling of philosophical perplexities. The work of philosophers may be nearer to that of aestheticians or art-critics than we suppposed; but still it can go forward. There are ways of discussing these things; that too is a language-game. I shall not dispute it. Yet once allow that it might be right to reject a proposition or mode of speech because the pattern has no place for it, and it must follow that it must sometimes be right to accept others on the same ground—that the pattern requires them. There is no inherent difficulty in the notion; the sense of what is necessary to complete the pattern is admittedly familiar in other contexts, and we need only recognize it at work in the present case. Yet here we have a way of seeing language that the whole bent of Wittgenstein's thought was opposed to.

For Wittgenstein there is no compulsion about language-forms, about the passing from one statement to another. An expression has as much meaning as we have given it: when doubt arises as to its right use in a new context, we can only refer to the language-game in which it has previously functioned. It has so much meaning and no more; its further application will be what we make it. No one part of our language can determine another; the use of our negative signs in a single negation cannot determine their use in double negation when we come to it; this latter either may affirm, or strengthen the negation. The parts of language are not connected by any piston-rods or natural laws—there is nothing of physics about its nature. There are many cases certainly where we find one development more natural than others; and some seem to us grossly unnatural. But those feelings—and here we are certainly treading slippery ground—though they may empirically determine what language we adopt, yet have no authority over its working. The only force here is that of rules, the accepted practice, which we may either deviate from or conform to. Beyond that we may construct languages as we will; to construct a language is to construct an instrument for a certain purpose, or to invent a new game. If we are to judge it by any objective criterion, presumably we must judge its performance with reference to the ends we have in view.

Now as against this, I shall claim that there is always more meaning in an expression than we have given it. For language is naturally a growing thing. I shall claim further that our feelings as to what is natural and unnatural, what belongs and what is foreign to a given linguistic system, are integral to its working. And we have seen that Wittgenstein himself implicitly allows as much; for our ability to appreciate what is foreign to a given system is what all his work must depend on. It is true that 'what is foreign' means there not what is merely wrong but what is senseless. It suffices however that our appreciation of pattern can form the basis of any judgement as to what is wrong or illegitimate in language; once the principle is granted, the restriction must be arbitrary.

'You grant that and the first point so you must grant this!' In this way, Wittgenstein writes, we can in fact compel a man to admit things.[1] Now first, we do not normally speak of compulsion except to a merely verbal admission; we get him to see it. He must see it for himself. Rational discourse is possible in that we and others see ourselves as compelled. And the question is not of fact but of right, as is soon established.

[1] *RFM*, i, 117.

Wittgenstein wishes to induce us to abandon certain modes of speech that, as philosophers, we have fallen into; to cease to feel perplexity over certain puzzles. But clearly it is not the change itself, however brought about, that will content him. It would not suffice if the linguistic therapist were to come equipped with some new effective drug, some sweet oblivious antidote, that effaced every vestige of our former philosophical distress. That point was noticed by Professor Wisdom long ago. What we require, then, must in some sense be rational conviction. It is not enough that we ourselves, or anyone, in fact abandon these modes of speech; it must be shown that it is fit or proper to abandon them. The assertion is a normative or evaluative one.

Here we are touching on a different side of a problem we have discussed in a previous chapter. The notion of normativity in Wittgenstein is explained solely in terms of reference to standards, and these standards he finds in existing practice. The doctrine necessarily raises doubts as to the status of Wittgenstein's own activity, for evidently he can have no standards to appeal to. Within existing language-games we can sensibly talk of right and wrong; and yet Wittgenstein's own activity takes us outside this monadism of language-games. It stands over and collates them. Indeed it claims to do no more than describe them, but the description, we find, is not a merely impartial or neutral one. Why it should not also correct and develop them, perhaps from the vantage point of its higher position modifying one in the light of another; or alternatively, leaving them to function in their own way in their appropriate spheres, develop another language more appropriate from this new point of view—that is not apparent. But these are questions which I shall have to return to.

Let us resume the argument at the point at which we left it. Wittgenstein requires that we appreciate the pattern or the working principle of a unique set of relations forming a language-game. We are to see that a given move is alien to the rest; and conversely it follows that we may come to see or feel that a given move is required by the rest, by the pattern. A word, I have claimed, always has more meaning than we have given it; for it demands this or that further application in new contexts, we feel this or that to be natural. A given use of the negation sign is compatible with different uses of the same sign in double negation; that may be granted. What is requisite is not that the demand of any one application or development should be absolute, but that divergences should be corrigible. And, of course, there is room, too, for a measure of elasticity. It is one thing to show us that in certain cases alternatives can be equally acceptable, for here we are still appealing to some principle of acceptability; it is another to suggest that in all cases any alternatives are—not indeed equally acceptable—but from a certain point of view unassessable, that it makes no sense to apply terms of evaluation to them. That is a contention which, in the nature of the case, cannot be established by means of examples of alternative courses that we evaluate as simply equally acceptable.

We find one or other development more natural but our feelings as to what is natural may conflict, and also, happily, can be changed. We may be made to see the pattern in a new way. That is what a large part of ordinary argument, not least Wittgenstein's own argument, is made up of. The error that stands in our way here is that of thinking of argument generally on the model of mathematical deduction. But for that, it could hardly be supposed that this process of 'assembling reminders', suggesting analogies and the like, was some serenely non-argumentative activity—a matter of mere neutral description, All this is argument *par excellence*; it is, outside the use of technical procedures and symbolisms in specialized fields, the kind of course we adopt when we want to convince anyone of almost any sort of disputable conclusion—to show that the methods of some new branch of Psychology have not made good their claim to be scientific, or that, given his record, John Doe is not the man to be entrusted with certain responsibilities. These are the ordinary uses of the term 'argument' as a little empirical investigation will show. The alternative course will be to revise the common usage of the word, giving it a better or perhaps a truer meaning; but that is hardly a course for Wittgensteinians.

It seems that for Wittgenstein our feelings, for instance, as to what is natural and unnatural, or perhaps rather our 'attitudes', determine the limits of any language-game; but within it they play no part. There we can only refer to the rules. A philosopher may feel that a word requires this or that application; but if our utterances are to have effective significance, we must look, not at the private feelings of the speaker, but rather at the public functioning of the terms. Certain feelings and also certain pictures may accompany the utterances of a given word; in effect these are nothing more than background music. Essentially they play no part in the game. Now, what Wittgenstein and others have said as to the variability, and in many cases the absence even, of all the experiential concomitants of speech, cannot be denied. It does not follow, however, that these experiences fill no function at all. Wittgenstein's picture may, I think, without misleading simplification, be said to show, first, divergences within language which can only be settled by reference to rules; and secondly, agreement as to those practices that constitute the language-game itself—which is based on agreement in attitudes. (This agreement as to attitudes perhaps involves feelings; for faced with the question of proceeding differently, we should feel it to be unnatural.) These questions of our feelings or attitudes are only raised, then, with reference to those procedures that constitute the very framework or basis of the language-game. But the truth, I suggest, is rather that throughout our use of language our feelings as to what is natural partly diverge and partly coincide; but that at every point, too, we seek, and feel it natural to seek, ways of bringing these divergent feelings into line. One way of achieving this end is that of reference to other accepted practices—which Wittgenstein sees solely and far too simply as an appeal to rules.

Here it may be objected that I am speaking of feelings where all the while I might have spoken simply of conduct. It is our practices that partly diverge, and that we change or adjust. We need not specifically feel it natural to do so, though we naturally do it. I maintain, however, that no account can make sense of this situation, of the progressive mutual adjustment of linguistic practice, from which all mention of experience itself is omitted. Perhaps an account that presents a picture in black and white—the comparison of practice to rules which they either conform to or diverge from—may with some slight plausibility leave it out. But even there it is unsatisfactory. A being might naturally conduct himself in one way, and then, on observing the conduct of others, stop, and thenceforth conduct himself differently. But suppose he had experienced no feelings or thoughts in the process—that we have some means of establishing that with certainty—then we should say, surely, that his behaviour had changed, but not that he had realized that he was wrong. The notions of right and wrong are only applicable where we are liable to be stopped by feelings of resistance or repugnance. For they require that we should be capable of realizing that we are wrong, which involves more than a change in behaviour.

It is true, certainly, that supposing someone repeats the premisses of the text-book example of a syllogism and concludes, 'Therefore Socrates is *not* mortal', one might say 'No' automatically, feeling nothing. If so, I may be asked whether that felt resistance which I speak of, which plays no part here, is not in principle altogether dispensable. Psychologically it is clear that feelings are prominent, consciousness comes in, in face of the strange or unexpected: we are held up by a feeling of resistance, and possibly led on to reflect. One may, however, imagine a language-game, involving sounds and movements much like those of our own more simple linguistic practices, where the players feel no such feelings at all. There, I should say, the word 'no' has not the meaning that it has for us; it is merely a mechanical reaction, like that of a plant whose petals close on being touched. And the words 'right' and 'wrong' also will lack the meaning we give them. Indeed in the complete absence of conscious feeling, it would surely be improper to talk of 'meaning' or to call the performance a linguistic practice at all.

But let us leave this imaginary and rather strained example. That the ordinary language-game of theoretical discussion—where doubts and slight divergences constantly arise, where different factors are weighed and compared, where the passage to some conclusion from certain premises seems to one speaker slightly unnatural, and is then set beside other similar linguistic practices for comparison—that all this should go forward, and experiential elements play no part in it is, I think, absurd to suppose. I shall be asked again, no doubt, whether that assertion is meant as analytic and necessary, or as merely an empirical one. I answer that I am not prepared to stretch imagination to the point at which I picture such a pattern of behaviour among automata. If they did or might behave in such a way all the terms of our language would need revision.[1]

---

[1] There is a further doubt that may be raised in this connexion: it may be said that I have no right to speak as if Wittgenstein endorsed any sort of behaviouristic theory of meaning; any such notion as that the concept of meaning might

There is one other context in which Wittgenstein brings feelings into his account, besides his discussion and dismissal of those distinctive feelings, that atmosphere that sometimes attaches to certain words. This further case is that of the feeling of giddiness that assails us, so he says, when certain philo- sophical questions are put; say, in dealing with the infinite or the infinitesimal, or when we are told that all perception is really of the percipient's own brain. These feelings, he says, are our danger signal; they show us that our language is out of gear. Now that may be granted—so long as we do not mistake the hint of a warning for a certainty. A feeling of giddiness may signify no more than that we are venturing on unfamiliar ground, on heights of speculation, perhaps, where our heads are not as yet used to the altitude. It is a common experience that a kind of problem that at first seemed to face one with a mere blank of bewilderment comes before long to offer clear bearings and an obvious foothold. But the point to insist on

exist as it does, though the language-users possessed no such experiences as they have at present, provided only that their behaviour was the same. For that is a possibility he could never seriously have envisaged; no meaning could have been given it. So much may be true. I claim, however, that the tendency of Wittgen- stein's work emerges clearly, whether or not he had himself acknowledged it. All his illustrations point to behaviour, to the public use of words, as the sole source of their meaningfulness; all his arguments are directed to the elimination of psychological factors as inessential. For instance, in the shopkeeper's game (*PI*, 1) he brushes away difficulties with the assumption that the players—in italics—*act* as he has described. Everything lies open to view, he says: but we are not told what they experience. And if they are robots then, I say, this is no language, and their 'words' are not in any ordinary sense meaningful.

Professor Findlay has suggested that Wittgenstein in his last work increasingly recognized the presence of psychological factors (*Philosophy* xxx (1955), p. 179). But I find no change in the real direction of his thought. Here as before, it seems to me, he is giving the theory a run for its money, though now perhaps a rather longer run, only to show its ultimate uselessness. The conclusion is to be estab- lished the more decisively. The discussion of the atmosphere of a word, which Findlay cites, (*PI*, p. 181) is surely not different in principle from the earlier discussion of the experience of reading and being guided (*PI*, 165-9).

here is the converse; that if a feeling of strangeness hints at something wrong, the feeling of fitness or necessity attaching to some logical or linguistic move witnesses to its rightness—with the same reservation as before, that a sound guide must not be taken for an infallible one. With no feelings as to what logical courses were right or wrong—as to what the pattern demands, in our previous terms—speculation would be at a standstill. Once again, the feelings of different people partly diverge; but this very divergence is dynamic, since we see it as calling for correction.

In general Wittgenstein presents in terms far too negative the part that intentional and psychological factors play in language. And though it may perhaps seem that nothing demonstrable follows from that, yet it throws the whole account out of true. For he is able to present right and wrong reasoning wholly as overt practice in accordance with recognized rules, and to treat that kind of demand that philosophical propositions may make on us, their compulsiveness, always as a sort of logical double-vision, a psychological factor, to be discounted. Yet the immediate obviousness or demandingness of any statement—in Philosophy or elsewhere—establishes its *prima facie* case to be heard. Let me repeat that Wittgenstein recognizes the feeling of strangeness as a signal to be taken notice of; and further, that he seeks to make us feel—I cannot see that any other term is more natural—the impertinence of certain elements in certain patterns. He cannot in consistency dismiss the feeling of appropriateness or necessity that also attaches to certain linguistic moves as always irrelevant or illusory.

I do not, of course, mean to convey the impression that these feelings I speak of need stand apart as discrete mental occurrences; often we could no more easily distinguish them than we can separate say, the menace of a thundercloud from its darkness. To feel that an element belongs to the pattern, to see that it belongs—either is a possible way of speaking. But the issues involved need not be pursued here; for it is our seeing or feeling—no matter which—that such and such a philosophical statement or development is obligatory, that Wittgenstein with his appeal to the past and existing application of words, to use and practice, wishes to rule out of consideration.

Closely connected with his treatment of feelings is his treatment of what he calls pictures, further subjective accompaniments of the use of language. These are the images that our forms of speech may bring with them—or pictorial ways of thinking which, never perhaps crystallizing as concrete mental images, nonetheless control the direction of our ideas. They too appear as merely obstructive things; as sources of confusion and perplexity. Wittgenstein seems to recognize no positive role at all as belonging to them; they are non-functional themselves, but block our vision of the functioning of words. He constantly appeals to us to ignore the pictures that we associate with our words and look instead at their use.

Now I cannot say in general that I find what seems to be the presupposition of this approach plausible: the suggestion that metaphors and models have no positive or functional role to play in our thinking. I cannot see what else thought can build on. But building is not Wittgenstein's interest; his trade is rather demolition. Here, as elsewhere, we find his characteristic anxiety to pin language down within the limits of its origins. He asks us to consider the situations in which words were first learnt; and clearly he wishes their career to end in the same circle in which it began. He is successful enough; if we are never to take account of our feelings as to what further applications the existing pattern demands, what further steps are necessary; if, too, we are never to use pictures or metaphors drawn from old fields of thought in tackling new ones, then creative thinking will certainly come to a stop—not only in

Philosophy but generally. Wittgenstein's whole treatment of language takes no account of the necessity or possibility of its growth; one may go further, it comes near to prohibiting it.

That pictures can imprison or mislead us is no good reason for not using them. The same may be said of those analogies between different regions of language which Wittgenstein identifies as the general source of philosophical perplexity; we think of one part in terms proper to others. No doubt the danger is real; but it does not appear why there should not be cross-fertilization—as between different cultures—as well as confusion. Here we come again on what I have called the monadism of Wittgenstein's treatment of language-games which has other consequences as well. Each complex of linguistic activities is taken by itself, and treated in effect as a virtually self-contained system. Within the game moves may be challenged and standards referred to; but the game as a whole has merely to be accepted. It has its own pattern of practices; and our great need is no more than to recognize the variousness of linguistic functioning. Indeed the sentence-schema '. . . has its own logic', has proved a godsend to contemporary philosophers.

Wittgenstein, in insisting on the pluralism of language-games, seems to lose sight of the unity of language. If these games are to be thought of as discrete, it must be rather as nuclei in a continuous medium; the matrix they are born of is one. It is true that linguistic systems develop in partial isolation, but they do not break away from their common origin. And they have the character they have, largely in virtue of that continued affiliation. In the catholicity of Wittgenstein's list of linguistic activities, such things as saying prayers and writing poetry are included; and Mr. Strawson has suggested that reading aloud to send an old man to sleep might equally legitimately find a place.[1] It seems that Wittgenstein's account of language or of language-games, each functioning by itself in its own way, leaves him no criterion for disqualifying from this name any system or pattern of activities—or perhaps we may say any involving marks or noises—no matter how remote from the assertion of what may be true or false. But language is unitary by reason of certain structural concepts that appear constantly throughout the plurality of its parts or departments; it is these that hold it together. Hence practices within one game can be said to conflict with those in another; a contingency Wittgenstein hardly seems to contemplate. Indeed such conflicts will not trouble us if we are always content to look at each game in isolation, to acknowledge the variousness of linguistic functions; so that to see how language functions here, and allow that elsewhere it may function differently, is all that we attempt. But what we shall then be left with is not one language, but a heap of languages.

We have found, for instance, that Wittgenstein maintains that philosophers fall into the error of believing a private language to be possible, thinking of the language of sensations on the analogy of the language of objects. We may certainly say, if we wish, that there are such things as sensations, and again that there are such things as material objects. But that in each case is to make a grammatical statement. The statement that there are material objects cannot have the same sort of force as the statement that there is a cat on the mat. The one falls within the language-game, and tells us something about what things there are in the world. But the other, on a Wittgensteinian view, can tell us no more than that a language-game of a certain kind is in fact played. For the notion of a material object defines that game; it is, so to speak, structural. It defines

[1] See his Critical Notice of *Philosophical Investigations* in *Mind*, lxiii (1954), p. 72.

a particular sort of linguistic practice. Grammar, Wittgenstein says, tells us what kind of object anything is; and, of course, there are many kinds of object—sensations as well as physical objects, for example.

If one says that there is both a cat on the mat and a mouse in the wainscot, one is making an ordinary existential statement about things; as I have said, it falls within the language-game. But to assert, as philosophers often assert, that there are both minds and bodies—or both experience and matter—is to do something different. That can amount to no more than saying that these two forms of linguistic activity, that in which we talk of sensations, of experience, and that in which we talk of material things, are in fact practised. I repeat the point, using the example of a conjunctive statement, because here, I suggest, the arbitrariness of Wittgenstein's presentation all but forces itself on us. It is the same notion of *existence* that occurs in both these two games; and again in the further language-games that we are playing when we stand outside and compare them. It is one and the same language we are speaking, using this term in different places; we are not dealing with disparate activities to be secluded in separate cells. Wittgenstein keeps them apart, assigns a different place and status to each, and gives the same word a different sense. To lay it down that existing usage is to be accepted as we find it and never tampered with is easier, perhaps, than to obey the injunction. Taking language as we find it, we should certainly suppose that these two existential propositions were the same in character. They are the same in form, Wittgenstein would presumably say, but different in function. Now the interpretation of their function is the point at issue, but let us grant it for argument's sake; it would seem that if so, existing usage must be badly in need of correction. For however freely we allow that there could be no language incapable of misapplication, surely the forms and functions of our terms should still keep up some sort of kinship. For when we use language in discussion or argument, assuming, for instance, the right to make such and such an inference here on the analogy of another somewhere else, it is formal likenesses we are bound to go on. The formal features of statements and arguments—their visible features, I do not speak of those forms symbolic logicians torture out of them—provide the whole steerage of discourse; they are what the progress of argument and of speculative inquiry generally depends on.

The monadism of Wittgenstein's account is bound up with his resistance to the recognition of any principle of growth as part of language; it serves to reinforce it. For he encloses our activities within discrete language-games beyond which there is no appeal. And we have already seen how he seeks to discredit the notion that one particular linguistic usage or practice may demand or necessitate others, disparaging those feelings on which this notion often rests; and to discredit too, those pictures and analogies that guide or govern the progress of new inquiry—that such progress necessarily builds on. This is a powerful concentration of ordnance; in face of this threefold battery, the advance of speculation may well be halted; thought may well be 'contained' within its existing frontiers. But we must recognize the extension of language, and the application of old terms in new spheres, as a necessary and normal part of its working. We must see it as part of the pattern of linguistic activity, even of grammar, perhaps, in Wittgenstein's sense, for it is a natural and general practice of language-users; and here as elsewhere one might answer, 'This is simply what I do.' And once we see that, we shall have no difficulty in granting, too, that philosophical usages, the inferences we make in Philosophy, the propositions we are led to, grow naturally out of the common body of language. This, too, is a linguistic activity.

'What language-game are you playing when you say that?' —for instance, that sensations are private. We may answer, the philosophical language-game; it has its own practices and patterns. Whom are we telling, and to what end? We are not concerned with any immediate practical end; we are engaged in a theoretical inquiry; and we are telling our fellow inquirers, other philosophers. A propos, it may be permissible to add that the notion of the privacy of sensations, and of the language in which we talk about them, will seem a less disastrous admission once the power of growth in language is recognized. A public language might grow out of private ones.

I have mentioned that Wittgenstein's list of legitimate linguistic activities is anything but exclusive; the poet and the punster are given a place. Only the metaphysician finds the doors shut on him. That seems arbitrary. But let us admit him: at least, it may still be argued, this use of language even though we recognize it along with the rest cannot be called descriptive. Its poetic character need not be denied it, but it cannot serve as an account of the world. Anyone but a Wittgensteinian can say that; Wittgenstein tells us that the different forms of description are infinitely various;[1] and presumably what is ostensibly a description may be taken for such until it is shown to be otherwise. I need not here, perhaps, launch on a discussion of the Verification Principle—even though Wittgensteinians and latter-day linguistic philosophers are apt to relapse into the bad habits of their positivist childhood, and fall back on it in an emergency.

But the working out the existing patterns of language may lead to interesting developments short of metaphysics on the grand scale: an example may be useful. At this stage I do not propose to open a new topic to be discussed at length; but it is worth mentioning one that Wittgenstein himself touched on in

[1] *PI*, 24.

his lectures—that of responsibility and free will. It is one that linguistic philosophers have not in general been happy in their attempts to tackle. For the most part they give us what Sidgwick and Moore called determinism—roughly, the view that 'I can' means 'I can if I choose'—and call it the dissolution of a pseudo-problem. Or else they give us illustrations—as of a chess-player who is free to set his piece on a range of squares, but not free to put it wherever he pleases—which seem, if anything, best calculated to illustrate traditional metaphysical indeterminism. Wittgenstein was more candid. In certain possible circumstances, he observed, given certain sorts of information, we might cease to use our present terms of praise and blame. The admission is crucial. I am not concerned to discuss the rightness of the conclusion; it suffices that it is acknowledged that reflection can lead to developments of language. And we may add that where developments conflict, more reflection will be called for. So the philosophical language-game comes into being.

One may play it or condemn it. But in face of the material offered us in *Philosophical Investigations*, it is hard not to ask what sort of linguistic activity Wittgenstein himself is engaged in; what game is this, and where are we to look for its rules? We met this difficulty in our previous discussion of logic and of the account that Wittgenstein gives of the normative. His own activity goes beyond all existing practice. His own aims are solely conservative and negative; but once the possibility of some such transcendent activity is allowed, of a game that stands over all other games, there seems to be no reason why it should be thus confined. He himself however has characterized his own work as descriptive, as that and nothing else: and surely, it may be said, the description of how people speak, the various ways in which they use language, is a linguistic activity to which a special status need no more be ascribed than to the

description of how they fight or how they fish. For Wittgenstein has no philosophical doctrines: as in the *Tractatus* here
also, he shows us things, he exhibits them, but says nothing.

It is a position that, if he really meant to hold it, can hardly
be maintained in the altered atmosphere of *Philosophical
Investigations*. It seems that Wittgenstein did after all hope to
influence linguistic usage—though the usage only of a limited
class of persons, specially occupied. He meant to influence the
usage of philosophers engaged in philosophizing. Now we have
already seen that it would not suffice that some merely practical efficacious way should be found of producing the changes
in question; a new serum would not serve. The means adopted
must be suited to influence rational beings.[1]

Here a further defence might be offered. Wittgenstein, I may
be told, never sought to influence anyone's mode of speech;
for was not he the philosopher who told us, 'Say what you
please'? Indeed he did. He let people say what they pleased
where he held that what they said made no difference. The
functioning of the words in our ordinary language-games gives
them their meaning; whether we opt for one or other philosophical terminology is immaterial. But then, between these
rival terminologies, which their exponents take to be rival
theories, there is no real difference. It is in this sense that Wittgenstein told contending philosophers that they might say what
they pleased; but sooner or later the split reappears. For though
you allow an idealist to lay it down if he chooses that matter is
unreal, yet he will hardly agree when you say that there is no
difference of belief between him and the materialist who says
that mind is unreal. Ultimately the attempt to make silence
speak, here as before, ends in absurdity.

---

[1] It might be said—and it is significant that it might—that all therapeutic
philosophers are guilty in principle of the naturalistic fallacy. They seek to get
an evaluation of usage out of what claims to be no more than description.

The philosophical proposition that matter is real amounts, we are told, to the proposition that the material-object language-game is played. Hence to say that matter is unreal would be in effect to assert that it is not played—and that is false. But there is surely a much more natural interpretation, even if we are bound to talk in these linguistic terms; to say this is to assert rather that the game—though it is—ought not to be played. And we have seen Wittgenstein himself seeking by rational means, and in the last resort by means not so very different from what philosophers have always used, to influence linguistic practice. He, it may be said, sought not to influence practice generally, but only that of philosophers; but the same is generally true of metaphysicians. Commonsense beliefs, they have held, function at a commonsense level. Their suggestion is not that the language of the man in the street should be changed, but that philosophers engaged in Philosophy should replace it by another that is in certain ways better.

A further point may be noticed in this connexion, unconnected with the main argument of the present chapter. We may recall that in Wittgenstein's view our language reflects or embodies our attitudes; it defines a way of life. It is surely natural to remark here that a theistic philosopher will have different attitudes from an atheistic one; and hence one may expect from him a different language. Wittgenstein holds that to treat people as we do—as people—implies the adoption of an attitude towards them; we look differently at objects we suppose to be conscious and rational. And that is much more than merely to hold certain beliefs about their minds. Now it is often said that to take a theistic view of the world is to see everything in it differently; that it is, at best, to see every action as a sacrament and every object as in some way divine. I do not know whether this is an attitude which we ought or ought not to take up—Wittgenstein allows no sense to such questions as regards attitudes. At least his philosophy seems to raise no special obstacle to it. Now those who see the world in this way do not go about their daily business differently from the rest of us. 'Who sweeps a floor, as for Thy laws', will still need to perform the same physical motions as those who assign cleanliness—or functional efficiency—the first place in the order of values rather than the second. Their ordinary language will presumably not be different; yet at the same time, we may expect, it will in some sense be doubled, be transposable, with another language that expresses another set of attitudes. The broomstick is not only a thing of use. To formulate such a language is one main task that traditional metaphysicians have set themselves.

Finally we may do well to say a few words of another line of criticism which Wittgenstein may seem to be exposed to—and indeed linguistic philosophy in general—but which, properly presented, it may claim to avoid. In reading Wittgenstein one may receive a recurrent impression that what one is being given amounts after all to a naturalistic metaphysic. His theme is the linguistic activity of people. That activity occurs in the setting of the material world; it involves bricks, apples, colour-charts and the like; it operates about or with reference to these things. But supposing we knew all there was to know about all this, about both the material setting and those complexes of human behaviour that constitute language, then there would be nothing else to learn. If you described a war or a cricket match, and saw how the different parts of the different players or fighters fit together, you would not need to speak of anything else; and these are the analogies we are given.

There are, I believe, traces of such a view in Wittgenstein's writings. It appears at its clearest in his treatment of Mathematics. It almost seems that his purpose here is to show how the analogy of the use of a standard object may enable us to under-

stand the function of mathematical statements, without postu-
lating anything beyond human utterances and behaviour—
behaviour as regulated by those utterances in appropriate contexts. But to present his position in this way is only to tell half
the story. There are other theses of his to be taken into account.
Grammar, he declares, tells us what kind of object anything is.
And presumably there are not only material things and sensations, but numbers, values, and perhaps much else; but in
saying so we are talking grammatically. There are so many uses
of language. In asserting therefore, that there exist material
objects, one no more succeeds in making an ontological statement, a statement about the contents of the world, than in
asserting that there are numbers or values. Both forms of discourse, both language-games, are among those that people
practise. It is true that in explaining the language-game of
mathematics say, Wittgenstein sets it in a world of material
things and shows how it functions in relation to them. But
perhaps in explaining the language-game of material things, he
may have occasion to use mathematical terms. And so, if you
will, he sets them in a world of mathematical objects. The argument cuts either way. In fact, he would probably claim that
this ontological model of the subject matter of meaningful
discourse is taken from an idealized notion of the name-
relation, the relation between a name and its object, which
is certainly one that can only exist as part of a more complex
setting.

Nonetheless there remains, about this point, a certain strain
in linguistic philosophy. In Wittgenstein's own account there
seem to be difficulties in treating 'sensation' and 'material
object' merely as grammatical terms, on a level with concepts
like number.[1] Other linguistic philosophers are certainly not
free from this naturalistic metaphysic I speak of: even Wisdom,

[1] Cf. above, pp. 93-5.

who sets out the issue the most clearly, in his treatment of what he calls the Idiosyncrasy Platitude, has moments of vacillation.[1] For a metaphysic is easier to disown than to disengage oneself from.

[1] Cf. below, footnote to p. 123.

V

Epilogue: John Wisdom

The contemporary influence of Wittgenstein's thought in English Philosophy would be hard to over-emphasize; its working, however, has been various. Generalizing, one may say that those philosophers who have carried linguistic philosophy forward, breaking new ground, have used rather than followed it; they have bent it to serve their own purposes. But there is one disciple who stands apart from the rest; the work of Professor Wisdom is truly Wittgensteinian, yet at the same time original and independent. It is this dual character that justifies some treatment of it here: indeed I shall claim that in some directions at least, Wisdom carries Wittgenstein's work further than he himself did, and faces its consequences more explicitly. We shall be better placed, therefore, to judge the balance-sheet of therapeutic philosophy with both before us. Besides Wisdom's approach is much less esoteric than Wittgenstein's, and his conclusions are perhaps easier to come to grips with.

We see in Wisdom something like a new application of Wittgenstein's ideas; we recognize the same forms there, yet cast, as it were, in a new medium; and the comparison may illuminate the work of both. The change that we find in turning from one to the other is hard to characterize in a word, and may emerge more clearly as we proceed. Wittgenstein, it has been pointed out, remained profoundly Germanic in his thinking; there is a Hegelian resonance in his utterances.[1] It is the feeling

[1] Cf. J .N. Findlay, 'Some Merits of Hegelianism', *Proceedings of the Aristotelian Society*, lvi (1955–6), pp. 1–25.

of strength and groping, of a mind working vastly with crude materials, that has disappeared in the anglicized version. Wittgenstein troubles us; his thought is disturbing. But with Wisdom we find ourselves at home again—an Englishman, at least, finds himself at home. His philosophy stands in the empiricist tradition, and his great concern is with the paradoxes of Scepticism and the problems of knowledge raised, principally, by Berkeley and Hume.

Scepticism leads, by reaction, to Metaphysics. It is in terms of these two broad movements or tendencies that positivistically minded philosophers in general have looked at Philosophy; they have seen Metaphysics less as a venture on its own account than as a last and desperate remedy for Scepticism, the cure being almost as bad as the disease. The task that falls to them, therefore, is to forestall metaphysical speculation by finding a prior and better answer to sceptical doubt. 'Can we know,' philosophers ask, 'and if so, how can we know, of the reality of ordinary objects about us; of the past; of the inward thoughts and feelings of other people?' These preëminently are the philosophical problems that Wisdom sets out to dissolve.

Such doubts, when philosophers raise them, are not practical or empirical. Wisdom dwells on the point at some length, but it is by now familiar and we may perhaps safely pass it more briefly. It is a totally different thing to raise suspicions say, of an all-but-perfect malingerer, and to bring up the philosophical problem of our knowledge of other people's minds. The philosophical problem arises because it seems possible to assert that, however a man may behave, now or in the future, his behaviour may belie his inward experience; and hence that we can never know for certain what he feels. It is in some sense possible to suppose that though he behaves at all times like a man in acute pain, yet he is secretly enjoying himself or feeling nothing.

Indeed the form in which the question is generally put is to ask whether other people may not be automata. It is clear that, conceived in this way, the doubt is one that no possible observation can resolve.

For that reason Wisdom regards it as suspect. Like Wittgenstein he treats philosophical questions and statements as being, in some sense, unreal or idle. His method too, is not to provide any straightforward answer, but rather to probe deeper into the question. We have seen that Wittgenstein broadly equates the meaning of words with their use. In the philosophical questions we have been speaking of the use of words has been covertly changed. Let us return to our example. A man in a hospital bed may scream and writhe; someone says, 'Perhaps he is not really in pain.' It is plain enough what the consequences of such a query will be if it is a real query, if we take the doubt seriously. We must re-examine the man's symptoms, perhaps inquire into his history, or watch him when he believes himself to be alone. Now suppose that someone asks the same question, but asks it, as we may say, 'philosophically'. We know at once that all that is irrelevant. The words are cut off, isolated, from all the effects they would normally have; and it follows that they cannot retain the same meaning.

This latter doubt, then, in no way affects the doubter's ordinary expectations; nor does it affect his behaviour. The philosophical sceptic shuts up his solipsism behind him as he closes the lecture-room door. He grasps as firmly at banisters, flares up as readily at insults and dreams as nostalgically of the days beyond recall, as any of his credulous companions. 'An odd sort of doubt,' is Wisdom's comment.

A similar but simpler example may make the point plainer. Philosophers raise doubts as to the unobservable objects of Science and call them in question no less than our ordinary beliefs concerning other people's experience. Now normally to

question whether there is an electric current in a given wire
will be to question say, whether the light-bulb attached to it
will go on, or the electric-train it usually drives will move when
the appropriate switches are turned. But here again the philosopher for all his doubts expects nothing different from the rest
of us. What is different, Wisdom says, is his use of language;
these words in his mouth do not bring with them the consequences they usually bring.

Our problem, then, is not to detect a fallacy in reasoning but
to understand an eccentricity in usage. When Richard Lovelace
wrote that the stone walls in which he found himself incarcer-
ated did not constitute a prison—rather, he said, he took them
for a hermitage—he was doing violence, and knew, of course,
that he was doing violence, to the English language. But philosophers are paradoxists who take their own paradoxes in
earnest. When a philosopher asks whether there is a current in
a wire that gives off sparks, drives trains and lights bulbs—so
that it is obvious that there is—what is required of us is not to
rack logic for some new subtler way of out-arguing him, but to
recognize a linguistic oddity for what it is.

Wisdom, in his articles on *Other Minds*, deals with three
principal cases in which we can be induced so to tighten our
usage that we come to doubt, or seem to doubt, beliefs that we
normally accept unhesitatingly. He deals with doubts as to
the reality of matter, doubts as to the reality of scientific objects, and doubts as to the reality of other people's inward experience. In each case, it appears, we normally make claims to
knowledge which, when they are tested, we cannot justify. In
each case there is a step from the grounds on which we base
our beliefs to the beliefs themselves. Our beliefs concerning
material things are based on our sense-data or sensations—so,
at least, it has often been said: our beliefs concerning scientific
objects are based on our observations of their 'effects': and our

beliefs concerning other people's minds are based on observation of their behaviour. In each case we are in some sense better assured of the ground than of the conclusion; and so, in some sense, it seems possible to accept the one and doubt the other. Now in ordinary life we make the passage without a qualm. The form of inference is different in each case, and in no case is it deductive: Wisdom's aim is no more than to bring us to see it and re-accept it for what it is. But this will appear more clearly in the sequel: it will be convenient first to approach these problems from a different point of view.

The questions we have been dealing with so far are those of the form, 'How can we have knowledge of such and such?' But the philosophers also characteristically ask questions of the form, 'What is the nature of such and such?' Philosophers in the past have sought to determine the nature of mind or of material things or of goodness; they have been led by Wittgenstein in recent years to concern themselves more often with the nature of statements about the mind, about material things or about goodness. We have seen that the difference between these two formulations is of paramount importance, but we may neglect it here. What concerns us at present is the peculiarity of the question in either form: philosophers, Wisdom says, always ask questions to which they already know the answers. A philosopher who asks about the nature of mind or of goodness already knows the meaning of the words; he is not ignorant like a child, nor yet like a scientist who asks what is the nature of a particular fluid. The facts are already before him. What kind of answers can he give? We shall do well to run over a few typical ones. What is goodness? It is a non-natural quality, some philosophers say, known by intuition or inspection as qualifying certain actual situations. Others deny that any such quality can be meaningfully spoken of; all facts must have sensible manifestations; moral utterances, therefore, do no more than express the feelings of those who utter them. Others again have asserted that moral discourse is in reality prescriptive; such statements do not describe states of affairs but are in the nature of imperatives. Others again seem to claim that they are after all factual in the ordinary sense: that to call something good is to say that it will conduce to the preservation of the race, or—a little more plausibly, perhaps—to the greatest satisfaction of wants. Value is satisfaction, we are told. Now all of these answers may be worth listening to: the first— for I have not set them in any chronological order—is valuable as correcting the others; the rest are illuminating, but strictly incorrect.

We must seek to see this more clearly. We shall find a great class of statements, apparently having the form that these accounts of the nature of goodness have, which no one will ever take exception to. For instance: 'A triangle is a three-sided figure'; 'A reptile is a cold-blooded animal'. And on this model we might construct an answer to our philosophical question with no greater difficulty: 'Moral statements are statements about good and evil; about how we ought and ought not to behave.' This is a faultless answer, but unhelpful; it tells us nothing that a person not ignorant of English does not already know. In Philosophy such answers are trivial. Certainly children, and also adults, are often ignorant: to one ignorant of the meaning of the word 'reptile', the statement that reptiles are cold-blooded animals may unquestionably be useful; it is also unquestionably correct. It is correct in virtue of the usage of these terms; the expressions forming the subject and the predicate are interchangeable. But the philosophical answers in the example we have looked at, have neither this authority nor this use.

It is necessary here to speak of what Wisdom calls 'the

legalist procedure'—a method of philosophical argument practised *par excellence* by Professor Moore. It is briefly this: take
any philosophical dictum of the form 'S is P'; find a typical
non-philosophical use, a use in ordinary language, of the term
S, and in the same way a typical use of the term P: indicate the
differences between them. Such differences will always exist
where the dictum is other than trivial. It follows that 'S is P' is
strictly false.

Let us return to our example. No one asserts as a literal
truth that 'moral statements are not statements', because this
is obviously false; it is self-contradictory. But suppose we say,
'Moral utterances—utterances about right and wrong—are
not statements': is this perhaps more satisfactory? No: it is
only more sophisticated. For usage is still our only court of
appeal; and, on consideration, we shall see that it is no more
correct usage in English to say that utterances about right and
wrong are not statements, than to say baldly that statements
are not statements. The impropriety is only less obvious; and
skilfully counterfeited banknotes are no more legal tender than
botched ones.[1] Of course this must be shown. I can offer no
more than a schema of Wisdom's views, all their force must lie
in the detail. But doubts will here surely arise: are such moves
as these really fatal when we are dealing with serious philosophical doctrines: do they serve against real and not merely
against pasteboard opponents? Let us see. We may at least take
the matter a little deeper. Let us suppose, then, that it is said
of moral sentences that they are—not certainly strictly imperatives—but conduct-guiding utterances resting ultimately on
personal decisions or choices. Now here I am concerned to

---

[1] The prettiest formulation, which exponents of such views are sometimes led
into, is, 'What would normally be called "moral statements" are not statements.'
Given their accepted account of logic, that *what are normally called statements are
statements*, is a necessary truth.

state only what I take Wisdom's answer to be. Further, the exponents of such doctrines as this share what is substantially
Wisdom's view of 'strict logic', that its appeal must be ultimately to usage. Let us grant this premiss, and the present
ethical doctrine breaks down in the end like the rest. We must
consider carefully the accepted usage of the terms 'decision'
and 'choice'. King Lear chose to disinherit his youngest daugh-
ter; he came to believe, but should we say that he chose to
believe, that he had done her wrong? Certainly the statement
before us is not overtly or flagrantly unorthodox; but it will
nonetheless break down under the persistent scrutiny of strict
legalism.

This process seems dreary. Are philosophers nothing but
pedants, peering at minutiae and red-pencilling nice linguistic
inexactitudes? We need not say so: for the legalist has mistaken
the nature of these philosophical utterances which he takes
exception to—forgivably, since those who make them generally mistake it themselves. He has failed to see their real use.
Philosophers are poets and paradoxists; they soar in free air;
they tell us that stone walls do not make prisons, that there are
no currents in wires that drive trains, that statements of such
and such kinds are not statements. The sophisticated moral
philosopher who disguises his own violation of usage—disguises
it also from himself—is already half infected with legalism;
his position is already undermined. It is better to be overtly
outrageous. But why, it may be asked, should it be thought
better: why should the false assertion that moral statements are
not strictly statements be thought valuable at all? For this
reason: when we speak of statements we naturally think first of
such statements as tell us of ordinarily observable states of
affairs, statements as that the cat is on the mat. Moral statements are very different from these; and it is held to be emi-
nently desirable that those moral philosophers who remain in-

sensible or ignorant of this difference should receive whatever jolting is needed to make them aware of it. The other theories we listed are also valuable: moral statements resemble imperatives; it is valuable that this resemblance should be emphasized; it has often been overlooked. But of course we must add that there are also differences: it is false that moral statements *are* imperatives. Hence the platitudes of legalism are of value too; the platitudes are corrective to the paradoxes. Once again we shall find likenesses that deserve notice between moral discourse and factual discourse concerning the satisfaction of wants: but here, as before, alongside the likenesses we must set the differences—differences which, in the present case, it has been the great service of imperativism to underline.

But now, as this process continues, it may occur to us that our original question has, in the course of asking it, already effectively been answered. We asked the nature of moral statements; and we will now have specified and enumerated in detail—supposing we had in fact travelled the course I have only indicated—all the various ways in which moral statements differ from, and all the ways in which they resemble, all the other kinds of statements to which they can be compared. We have given the fullest possible answer in the only terms in which it could be given. What other or better description of moral statements could there be? Yet we have been told nothing but what we already knew; the dialectic of paradox and counter-paradox returns us at last to the platitude from which we set out: moral statements are moral statements—this is the only strictly true answer that the question admits of. But such an answer, if it were offered before this course of inquiry had been embarked on, would have been dismissed, and rightly dismissed, as vacuous; when we return to it in the end, when the whole circle has been traced, we shall be content to rest here and ask no more. Yet if in one sense we only rediscover what we already knew, yet we see it now with a new and deepened insight. The effect of our inquiry is to set this one concept that concerns us in its place on the conceptual map we have drawn. We set it among its logical neighbours.

Wisdom, like Wittgenstein, calls his philosophy descriptive. And a question of the form, 'What is the nature of such and such?' seems, certainly, to require a description for answer. But the kind of answer that is in fact expected and given, a philosophical account—this is the term most used—is more often thought of as being simultaneously descriptive and explanatory. To explain a thing in philosophy is to exhibit it as necessary or possible. We may see this in the case we have been looking at. Moral utterances are said by some philosophers to be imperatives; and the point of this way of describing them is to explain the possibility of their meaningfulness—such utterances being neither empirical nor analytic. The point, to take a similar example, of describing necessary truths as tautologies is likewise to explain the possibility of such knowledge: knowledge of truths that neither require nor admit of empirical testing. Both descriptions are false: both explanations, therefore, are unsuccessful. If we can only grasp this failure properly we shall have got hold of the crux of our problem. We shall have taken the step from analysis to what lies beyond analysis, which even Wittgenstein only falteringly took, and which certain Oxford philosophers—speaking from a Wisdomite point of view—have since widely gone back on.

We are better placed now to turn back to the epistemological issues that we raised at the start. We saw that there are various types or categories of discourse that Wisdom distinguishes: for instance, there is discourse concerning material objects, discourse concerning scientific objects and discourse concerning other people's minds. Now, further, each linguistic category defines an ontological one. When we are asked in philosophy the nature of a such and such, we can only answer by specifying the ways in which it can be known. For there are different modes of argument, different forms of support appropriate in each case; we give reasons, but the reasons have a different bearing or a different weight. Hence of these two different forms which philosophers' questions may take—we may ask the nature of such and such, or we may ask how we have knowledge of such and such—both must meet the same ultimate answer. We are not in search of new evidence in the ordinary sense; we can only deal with either question in the end by recapitulating in full the relevant modes of logical procedure—relevant in this category of discourse. Thus the ontological question we were faced by, identifies itself with what seemed to be different, the epistemological one.[1]

We may give these general remarks application. Chairs and tables are known to us by observation in the ordinary sense; but one cannot know of scientific objects in this way. One can feel one's own feelings but not another man's. The occurrences belong to different categories. And with this established we can reassess the sceptic's strangely plausible argument, for it now lies open to view. We can now look into it and see how it works. What he asks for, in effect, is to know the objects of one category in ways appropriate only to those of another; we touched on this before. But categorical objects are defined by the ways in which they may be known; hence his demand is, in effect, that we transfer them from the one category to the other; and in the outcome, he is still left empty-handed. 'I could know that you have feelings', he insists, 'if and only if I could feel them.' Then they would be his own feelings and no longer mine. The sceptic legislates a whole category of discourse out of operation. The lesson, however, that we may learn from seeing this has a wider application; our concern here is with

[1] Cf. *PP-A*, p. 229.

philosophical explanation in general. What needs here to be insisted on is that the counter-arguments that scepticism is met with—those philosophical accounts of different modes of knowledge, the explanations or explanatory descriptions we have been looking at—fall into the same trap that the sceptic, his own victim, is caught in. An example is the argument from analogy as applied to the problems of knowledge of other people's minds: this argument is intended to rebut the menace of scepticism; it seeks, and as many hold succeeds in its attempt, to explain the possibility of such knowledge.

We must briefly examine its working. There are many things we might normally, with the warrant of usage, claim that we know by analogy. One may know that an acorn will, in suitable circumstances, develop into an oak tree, by analogy with the observed development of other acorns. In due course one may observe the young tree; Methuselah might observe it in its prime. Thus we know the character of analogical arguments in general: and to claim that it is also by analogy that we know of the feelings of other people must surely be, on the face of it at least, to claim to know them in the way in which we know of the future development of acorns. And this claim is false: we do not know of them in this way. I have said that we may presently observe the young tree; we shall never observe another man's feelings; neither Methuselah nor yet Madame Sosostris can do that. Hence if we are to say that it is by analogy that we know of others' minds, we shall need to add the qualification that it is a peculiar species of analogy—its peculiarity being that the second analogue is never directly observable.

We started with two types of argument: first the ordinary kind of argument from analogy, both analogues being in principle observable; and second, that kind of argument that gives us knowledge of others' minds. To the latter the sceptic raised objections: the feelings of others are never observable. He is met by the argument from analogy; but we are soon forced to recognize that the analogy is of a special kind in that the second analogue is not directly observable—which was precisely the peculiarity the sceptic complained of in the first place. We may say that we have found that there is not one, there are two types of analogical argument; little turns on the description; but we are only calling the old differences by new names. It is the same point which we always halt at: the apologist with his explanation, no less than the sceptic with his proof, cannot accept the thing before him for what it is; but in the end knowledge of others' minds cannot, any more than anything else, be explained or made intelligible by turning it into some other thing which it is not. It may in some ways be like, but in other ways it is also unlike, our knowledge of the future development of acorns; in the last resort it only *is* itself.

It is no less false that moral statements are imperatives: it is true, however, that they in certain ways resemble imperatives. By pointing out these resemblances, one describes them—or rather, makes a contribution to their description, of which other ethical theories contribute the rest. This false description fails, being false, to explain the possibility of the meaningfulness of such statements; yet it may be that after the attempt, and the failure, we shall be more ready to accept them, in their own right, without qualms. For, of course, that we may make statements about the rightness of actions, which, like all statements, are meaningful, is only a platitude. Thus, Wisdom writes, explanation falls back into redescription. And in the end we may come to be satisfied that this description is all that we can ask for.

In the first of his articles on *Other Minds* Wisdom's great emphasis is on the empirical emptiness of philosophical scepticism. But that is only the first step in clarification. Later he states the form of philosophical problems differently. Philosophers, in face of any category of discourse, characteristically ask, 'Are these "reasons" really reasons?' The sceptic denies that we can know of certain objects—whatever sort is in question. He points out that the kind of reasons which we support our claims to such knowledge with are different from those we use elsewhere. When he asserts that we can never know of others' minds, or never talk objectively about right and wrong, his arguments are in fact directed to establish the inadequacy of everything we usually would call a reason in favour of any belief in these fields: these, he argues, are not really reasons. The anti-sceptical apologist of commonsense—vindicating the rationality of ethical discourse, or the possibility of knowledge of other minds—tells us that after all these reasons are reasons: but he does it at the expense of a vain attempt to reduce arguments of one category to those of another. To justify any body of beliefs, in the last resort, could only be to recapitulate in full our ordinary reasons; to retrace at length the steps we have taken in arriving at them.

Wisdom remarks, in discussing the work of an outstanding exponent, or sometime exponent, of reductionism, that whereas by deductive argument we can pass from statements of one type to others of the same type, we cannot pass from those of one type to those of another.[1] Thus we may pass from sense-data statements to other sense-data statements by deduction, but not from these to material-object statements, from factual statements to other factual statements, but not from these to ethical ones. These remarks dovetail, with the precision that characterizes Wisdom's thought, with our present findings. A type of statements is defined by the ways in which they can be verified. If two statements can be verified in the same way, they belong to the same type. If we can pass deductively from one statement S, to another S_1, then any process that confirms

---

[1] A Note on *Language Truth and Logic*, *PP-A*, p. 246.

or verifies S must with the same strength confirm or verify S_1. It follows that they belong to the same type. Types, to put it differently, may be defined as deductively irreducible modes of discourse. The philosopher's undertaking, to justify a given mode of discourse, to explain its possibility, cannot therefore be achieved by deduction. Each category is what it is and nothing else: just this, we have seen, is the ground of complaint against it. Deductive argument, we suppose, might carry us from this one category of discourse, which for the moment we are uncritical of, to this other, which we are immediately troubled over; it might explain how the latter can be possible. We deceive ourselves: if we could succeed we should find ourselves, like Alice, back at our starting-point; we should find that it was the old category we still had on our hands. Philosophy requires, not deduction, but rather revelation. It is with no slackening of logical stringency that Wisdom says so, this must by now be evident; it is no invitation to day-dreaming. We tell ourselves, perhaps, that our scrutiny of the sceptic's reasoning has even now not been rigorous enough, or our analyses not sufficiently subtle. It is not so. We would gladly ransack logic till the end of time; but, Wisdom would perhaps say, sometimes the simpler course is also the harder one—to take hold of the object before us.

It will be seen that Wisdom's philosophy is, after its own fashion, dialectical; for a philosophical inquiry in his presenta- tion of it appears as progressing through a succession of part- truths—all finally to be taken up into a reapprehension or reacceptance of the whole. Now a dialectical approach to Philosophy is always naturally a historical one. And, in spite of Wisdom's apparent indifference to the History of Philosophy, we find it so here. He applies it to recent philosophy in Eng- land; especially, he concerns himself with the opposition of

Realism and Analysis—an opposition that the Therapeutic Method serves to resolve, thus completing the triad. He uses Wittgenstein, we may say, to mediate between Russell and Moore.

By Realism Wisdom means a philosophy which works with non-natural qualities, subsistent universals and the like—metaphysical entities taken in each case as ultimate. Such doctrines have been widely held, but they have also been consistently opposed. These entities have always aroused suspicion among philosophers of a different sort; they are derided as 'mysterious' or 'ghostly'. The metaphysical thesis accordingly calls up its analytic antithesis; attempts are made to eliminate them by analysis. Universals, for instance, are analysed into resemblances of particulars; 'good' is declared to be a *quasi* imperative—and not therefore the name of a non-natural quality. Now the realist will always plausibly claim, according to Wisdom, that such analyses break down; and in a sense he is right. An analytic proposition such as that a triangle is a three-sided figure is valuable in Mathematics but ultimately trivial in Philosophy. We may be told, perhaps, that 'good' means 'what ought to be done'; but such an analysis—even granting that it is otherwise acceptable—has failed to eliminate the normative notion of 'ought'. Briefly the position is this: either we analyse normative notions such as goodness into something other than goodness—say, pleasure, or the survival of the race—in which case the analysis breaks down; or alternatively, if we produce a truly analytic proposition, we will not have succeeded in eliminating the notion we claimed to have analysed. The realist, therefore, will always maintain that his metaphysical entities are vindicated, that nothing else will suffice. Yet the persistently renewed search for satisfactory analyses, in face of recurrent failure, requires explanation nonetheless; Wisdom asks why it is that the Realist's ultimate objects and entities are still felt to be suspect. He answers that they are only commonsense dressed up.[1] The peculiarity of these metaphysical theses is one we are by now familiar with: they seem to represent startling discoveries; in fact they tell us nothing but what we already know. Universals are subsistent entities, we are told, instantiated in particulars, but only directly known to intuition: goodness is a non-natural quality, unanalysable into anything else; and so too with material objects, numbers and so on. Each is unique. But might we not as well have said in the first place, with fewer and shorter words but the same effect, that goodness is goodness, numbers numbers, tables tables—and that each is unique. The metaphysician's statements are not false or inaccurate; they are perfectly invulnerable to logical criticism. The objection to them is that they are pompous and empty.

Wisdom in this connexion quotes the saying of Butler that Moore made famous, 'Everything is what it is and not another thing.' This maxim, which he christens the Idiosyncrasy Platitude, is the motto of the realist metaphysician; by its means he can always confute those logical reductions and analyses put forward by his nominalistic opponents. Now we have seen that Wisdom, in a certain sense, must himself endorse the Idiosyncrasy Platitude;[2] it is true that everything is what it is, a philosophical truth. What he insists on is only that it is platitudinous; philosophical truths, we know, are all platitudes. Hence Wisdom's position is at once identical with that of the realist metaphysician and worlds removed from it. For the metaphysician believes that in discovering the hitherto undreamt of existence of this realm of transcendental entities, he has come on something striking and strange; whereas Wisdom believes that he has made no discovery more remarkable than that of Polonius, that true madness consists in being mad. For

[1] *PP-A*, p. 85.　　　　　　[2] Cf. *OM*, p. 53.

these metaphysical modes of discourse ray no more than we all said, and thought nothing of, in the language we spoke before ever we learned to speak like philosophers. And on the other hand, once one grasps that the existence and the uniqueness of such entities is in fact not a discovery but a commonplace, then the uneasiness that sends the analyst in search of the means of their elimination will also, on its side, disappear.

The value of Realism for Wisdom is only as a corrective to Reductionism. No one category of discourse is wholly analysable into another; each has its own role which no other can precisely fill. The logic say of 'good' and its synonyms is unique, and that is what the Realist in effect insists on; for the whole ground he can give for his postulated metaphysical entities is the failure of reductive analysis.[1]

Here, as elsewhere, Wisdom does not seek to answer the questions philosophers put, but rather, like Wittgenstein, to eliminate the need to ask them. The broad similarity of their views is clear, but there are real and radical differences as well. And at this point, before passing on to any general criticism, we shall do well to attempt some comparison between the two.

[1] The passage in *Other Minds* III (p. 73), where Wisdom speaks of the more-than-logical issue that the analyst fails to face, deserves to be quoted.

'You remember it was said—to stop the worry it was said—"He has the measle germ" just means "He will give all the measle-reactions." Now this is incorrect. But that again is not the point. The point is that this answer is too soothing. Or rather not too soothing—nothing could be that, everything's absolutely all right in metaphysics—but it's too sickly soothing. It's soothing without requiring of us that act of courage, that flinging away of our battery of crutches, which is required in order to realize that everything's all right. This phenomenalist answer soothes without demanding this change of heart only by soothing deceptively and saying that this alarming hippopotamus is only a horse that lives in rivers. It's true that the hippopotamus is quite O.K. and not at all carnivorous and won't hurt anybody who treats him right—that is treats him like a hippopotamus has to be treated; but it's a mistake to soothe people by telling them that he's a horse because, though that may soothe them for the moment, they will soon find that to treat him like a horse is not satisfactory . . .'

Wisdom's great concern is, as we have seen, with Philosophical Scepticism, and hence with the reasons—what we
normally call reasons—for our ordinary or commonsense beliefs. Both philosophers appeal to the ordinary use of language
—from which, so they claim, philosophers have diverged. But
Wittgenstein's 'language-games' become, in Wisdom, types or
categories of discourse. Wittgenstein asks the use of a word,
and tells us to think of it as a tool. Wisdom asks what counts as
a reason for whatever type of belief is in question, or what
weight a given reason carries there; for what carries more
weight in one category may carry less or none at all in another.
Thus Wittgenstein's emphasis on usage is preserved, yet at
the same time is curiously altered. And further his whole treatment of normative discourse, in terms of the appeal to paradigms or rules, has no place in Wisdom's work; in a sense it is
forestalled or undermined, for 'reason' is already a normative
notion. Wisdom's position is very clear as to this point:
normative discourse in his account is quite simply one category
among others, and as such must ultimately be accepted. It cannot be explained or analysed in terms of anything else more
fundamental.

It may be questioned, however, whether Wittgenstein meant
to attempt such an analysis; he never claimed that it can. Here
we are led on to the second and deeper difference between them.
It is true that Wittgenstein explicitly tells us that our task is to
note, not to explain, this or that language-game.[1] Yet it is
hard not to feel that his own work overstepped the prohibition.
For we are to look at the uses of words, to get a clear view, to
see them as tools; and unless their behaviour is in some way
to be made intelligible or explicable here in terms of their function, of the job that they do, it is hard to see what we will gain
by the inquiry. The last example will serve: given a world that

[1] *PI*, 655.

contains nothing but natural objects, tables and people and
pains, how are we to explain the meaningfulness of normative
terms? It is at least no unnatural interpretation of Wittgenstein's account—in terms of paradigms and rules—to suppose
that it is designed to solve some such problem as that. It admits,
to be sure, of other interpretations too,[1] yet on those interpretations, I am tempted to say, the labour and stress of the argument seems hardly to be justified by the outcome: the net gain
is slight.

In Wisdom we meet reasons not uses. Wisdom repeatedly
acknowledges his debt to Wittgenstein and refers to his work,
but not, I think, to his favourite analogy of a tool—an analogy
which seems to presuppose or hint at the question, 'Why do
we use language at all?' There are many, various considerations we adduce which we normally reckon as reasons for our
different commonsense beliefs: and on Wisdom's account philosophical 'explanation' can do no more ultimately than recapitulate them in their entirety. We cannot demonstrate from any
more fundamental position that these reasons, as we call them,
are really such: no one category of discourse can be justified
or explained in terms of another. Wisdom's treatment of the
Idiosyncrasy Platitude makes explicit this central point, on
which Wittgenstein seems to waver. Wittgenstein taught philosophers to ask linguistic questions instead of ontological ones,
and so doing, Wisdom claims, he marvellously transformed
them.[2] Instead of seeking to determine the nature of matter or
of mind or of value, they were led to concern themselves with
the material—or mental or evaluative—uses of language. And
yet, notwithstanding the transformation, the questions still
remain, and they are no more answerable in the new form than
the old. We now ask not 'What is value?' but 'What is the
evaluative use of words?' The only answer, we have seen, is to

[1] Cf. above, pp. 100–2.   [2] *PP-A*, p. 118.

describe it at length; there is no account of it that will reduce it to more basic terms. In the end we must accept it for what it is.[1]

Finally it is necessary to repeat that the outlining of Wisdom's therapeutic method in Philosophy must be very different from its actual practice. All the force of the process is in the detail. His method is simply to recapitulate, in all their complexity, the ordinary uses of language. Philosophers formulate and demand that we choose between different classifactory systems—Wisdom uses the metaphor of a net spread over the 'manifold of the individual'[2]—they do not point to different

[1] I have said that Wisdom's account of the Idiosyncrasy Platitude serves to make these points explicit; but in other respects it seems rather to go back on Wittgenstein's findings—though I do not believe he intends it so. The questions involved are very complex and I have not space to treat them adequately. Roughly, we are to ask whether each linguistic category in this account determines an ontological one. The realist asserts, for instance, that goodness is a non-natural quality; and Wisdom replies that that, in effect, is no more than a platitude. For it amounts to no more than saying that goodness is goodness, that a given category of discourse is what it is. But then, we must ask, what of Wittgenstein's work on the fallacy of treating words generally as names? 'Goodness', he would say, is not the name of any sort of quality; and so far, the realist is plainly in error. The problem becomes acute with reference to the two great categories of mental and physical discourse. For Wittgenstein this difference is a grammatical one only. But the realist—here also a dualist—who asserts that there are both minds and bodies, or better, both experience and behaviour, says and means that there are two distinct kinds of entity or process in the world. If Dualism is strictly right but platitudinous—as Wisdom once told me in conversation—then Wittgenstein's account must be paradoxical and wrong. The trouble arises, perhaps, from the false parallelism of say, mathematical and material-object language, with behavioural and experiential language; if the former difference is 'grammatical' the latter is something different. As to Wisdom's position, I cannot but suspect that he has not sufficiently earnestly asked himself whether he believes in ontological categories to match his linguistic ones or not. Where he speaks of it (*PP-A*, p. 37) he vacillates easily, even ironically, between talk of 'different sub-languages within a language' and ontological talk of 'different categories of being'.

[2] Cf. *PP-A*, p. 119. The metaphor was, of course, previously used by Wittgenstein in the *Tractatus*; I do not know whether it has a yet earlier history.

facts. What they oppose are different ways of organizing or describing the ordinary material of discourse. It is here that Wisdom demands a return to the concrete; for as regards this common, concrete material there is no dispute. There is no dispute as to the occasions on which, in daily life, we claim knowledge or confess ignorance of the thoughts and feelings of other people, nor as to the manner in which such claims are supported. The same is true in those other related fields that science and sense perception are concerned with. And it is possible to set out all these facts, the exact features of each separate case, and the likenesses and differences between them, in terms that can hardly give rise to controversy—in 'aseptic' terms, as Wisdom calls them. Here there is no quarrel; yet it is this, the familiar concrete material that makes the content, gives the meaning, of those philosophical abstractions which seem to stand in irreconcilable opposition. We commit ourselves with regard to such abstractions; we take our stand, and defend them tenaciously, like flags. But so long as the same army fights the same battle, the flag it fights under is immaterial. The way out of the impasse of abstractions is to recapitulate, to recall in detail in the way we have spoken of, in aseptic terms, all our ordinary ways of talking in ordinary situations; it is found in exhaustive description and nothing else.[1]

[1] I have outlined only that part of Wisdom's thought that may be seen as a recasting of Wittgenstein's. Latterly new themes have claimed his attention. He has recognized that not only metaphysicians are (in his sense) paradoxists. He speaks of 'reflection' which leads to propositions that are neither analytic nor synthetic, in the positivist's sense, but show us new patterns in familiar material; and scientists no less than philosophers may do that. So doing, too, they may sometimes collide with accepted forms of speech, with old ideas embodied in old usage. This more recent work of Wisdom's is of great interest; though it seems undeniable that its tendency is often to take the sting out of some of his own earlier arguments. These views are most fully expounded in the four articles entitled Philosophy, Metaphysics and Psycho-Analysis (*PP-A*, pp. 248–82).

.   .   .   .   .

In the previous chapter I dealt with the main difficulties that I find in Wittgenstein's philosophy: I shall conclude with a few critical comments on the therapeutic method as presented by Wisdom.

Wisdom's starting-point in his articles on *Other Minds* is clearly the analytic-synthetic dichotomy as used by those philosophers whom we may call classical positivists. His first move is to distinguish statements expressing 'natural' doubts that involve empirical consequences from those that do not—that have, in effect, been made or taken as analytic. The classical positivists, however, quite simply defined factual meaning in terms of empirical verification—and hence deduced the meaninglessness of all would-be factual utterances involving no empirical consequences. But that is an unsatisfactory procedure: a doctrine packed into a definition, advanced in this form, is both provocative and vulnerable. It draws fire and is unable to meet it: a definition is something no one can be obliged to adopt. Wisdom, therefore, found a different way, he sought to steer a neutral, non-belligerent course; his vocabulary was to carry no contraband. He set out to do no more than to describe—to lay before us in the fullest detail, in the least tendentious terms—the actual familiar workings of ordinary language. These sentences, he shows us, function thus and thus, they do these and these empirical jobs; those sentences do certain logical jobs, their functioning is also set forth. And lastly certain other classes of sentence function, observe, in neither of these ways, and, to describe it non-aseptically, do no job at all. Wisdom never enters the dialectical arena; he is no advocate as Ayer is. Like Mark Antony, he tells us nothing but what we ourselves already know; he leaves the facts, like Caesar's wounds (poor, poor dumb mouths) to speak for themselves.

The facts indeed speak, with a little prompting. The use of

aseptic language is easier to recommend than to practise, and in Wisdom's case, proves to be compatible with distinguishing between questions that are 'practical and settlable' and questions that are 'academic and idle'.[1] Clearly the mere form or actual usage of any expression does not tell us whether it is analytic or synthetic; otherwise Wisdom himself would be out of work. Its status is to be elicited by reflecting on speculative situations, even on queer half-imaginable worlds—involving confluent streams of consciousness and the like. All this is still offered as 'descriptive'. The importance of the argument for us is that it puts it beyond doubt that Wisdom's own position was reached by some philosophical method other than that which he himself advocates—a damaging criticism, surely, of a philosopher whose central thesis is above all methodological. Wisdom, like any scientist bringing his hypothesis to the facts, conceives first a general classification of forms of language, and then—rightly, for what else could he do?—manipulates the concrete material to see if it might not be made to fit. Metaphysicians do the same; they, however, are not pre-committed to the doctrine that a concrete redescription in neutral terms, putting all abstract preconceptions on one side, will reveal the emptiness of all such issues. The point is worth insisting on, because it seems to be supposed that the use of theories or hypotheses, which are first framed and subsequently tested, is not only characteristically but exclusively the procedure of scientists. It is true, of course, that philosophers do not test their theories by observation; but they conceive systems, and then try to show that the familiar material of experience accords with them; or, alternatively, they look for possible situations that cannot be accommodated in the systems of their rivals. But the pattern—the framing first, then the application of theories—is the same.

[1] Cf. *OM*, p. 12.

Wisdom leans still more heavily on his doctrine of language-categories than on the traditional analytic-synthetic dichotomy. We have seen that the sceptic seeks to verify statements from one category in ways appropriate to those of another; he seeks, for instance, to verify statements about minds in ways appropriate to statements about bodies, and so doing necessarily fails. Each has its own types of procedure. But if no other category existed, to which other procedures belong, these statements could never be verified. Scepticism would then appear not as an absurd position but an unanswerable one.

Now given any particular subject-matter, one may naturally suppose that it admits of division in various ways; Wisdom, when he gives the matter his direct attention, speaks as if the variety of such systems were indefinitely large.[1] Further not all of them will be mutually compatible: some will conflict with others, and disputes as to their relative merits will arise. But here we are brought back to our starting-point: the *raison d'etre* of the descriptive method was nothing but the circumvention of disputes such as this—disputes between alternative abstract ways of presenting the same ultimate stuff. And such disputes, however we describe them, make up the ordinary activity of philosophy.

Wisdom seems to write as if his own categorization of forms of factual statement were uncontroversial; or emerged from a mere description of the material. But such a claim can hardly be maintained. In fact he has his own principle of classification, namely observability, and it is clearly always arguable that others may prove more important or fundamental.[2]

[1] Cf. *PP.A*, pp. 118–19.
[2] Wisdom's categories are (i) sensations or sense-data, (ii) material objects, (iii) scientific objects, (iv) other minds: that is, roughly, entities that are directly observable, those that are observable in the ordinary, non-philosophical sense, those that are only observable through their 'effects', and those that are directly observable 'only to one' (*OM*, p. 226). Let us take the case of scientific objects.

The truth is that the facts we describe will receive their character partly from the system in terms of which we describe them—as indeed appears clearly enough in Wisdom's would-be aseptic descriptions of language-forms. These systems, in turn, must be assessed as serving better or worse to accommodate their material. For objects assigned to different categories must be differently distinguished from objects within the same category; and in the merely ground-level description these differences will never appear. Given two objects *a* and *b* in one category, and two in another, *z* and *y*: *a* and *b* will differ from *z* and *y* in a different way from that in which *a* differs from *b*. A table differs from a table-sense-datum in a different way from that in which a card table differs from a kitchen table. And this categorical difference arises from the demands of the system as a whole; if disputes break out here, it is to theoretical considerations that we must appeal. Let us take a third object *m*. The character *m* has will differ radically according to the category to which we assign it; but from the point of view of a ground-level description there is, perhaps, only a continuous series, *a*, *b*, *m*, *y*, *z*. Suppose that after all we were to accept Wisdom's own system of categories; that could not be because it emerged in a mere description of the facts—no system can emerge in such a way. It must be, if at all, because it on the whole has fewer difficulties, and serves to provide for and

Wisdom speaks much of what he calls invisible germs; they are almost his stock example of scientific unobservables. Now it is true in many cases that a single virus cannot be observed; and that may serve to relegate such viruses to a different logical category from those that can. On the other hand a colony of such viruses may be observable; hence the colony will belong to a different category from the individual. The analogy of a crowd of people visible in the distance where one alone is out of sight is so obvious that it seems perverse to ignore it. But now already we are engaged in a dispute as to what principles of classification we are to adopt. Observability alone, then, is not sufficient; no one principle can be taken for granted.

handle its material with less strain than its rivals. But all this has still to be determined.

We need not deny all utility to the descriptive method, the 'return to the concrete'. In certain cases it is undoubtedly salutary, when an argument is stuck in its high abstract terms, to re-examine the concrete material in dispute; sometimes we can break the impasse in this way. But the expedient has no infallible efficacy. At other times we shall need new ideas, not a re-examination of the old; not retrenchment but rather creativeness. Intellectual invention and argument in Philosophy can never be replaced by mere description.

Index